**In the Shadow of the Swastika**

13 Nov 2007

TO IRVIN,

FROM The son of

"ENRICO"

# In the Shadow

# of the Swastika

## Hermann Wygoda

### Edited by Mark Wygoda

### Foreword by Michael Berenbaum

University of Illinois Press

Urbana and Chicago

Publication of this book was supported by the
Sheldon Drobny Family Endowment for the
University of Illinois Press.

∞ This book is printed on acid-free paper.

Library of Congress Cataloging-in-Publication Data
Wygoda, Hermann, 1906–1982
In the shadow of the swastika / Hermann Wygoda ; edited by
Mark Wygoda ; foreword by Michael Berenbaum.
p.   cm.
Includes index.
ISBN 0-252-02382-x (cl. : alk. paper)
ISBN 0-252-07139-5 (pbk. : alk. paper)
1. Wygoda, Hermann, 1906–1982.
2. Jews—Poland—Biography.
3. Holocaust, Jewish (1939–1945)—Personal narratives.
4. World War, 1939–1945—Jewish resistance.
5. World War, 1939–1945—Underground movements—Italy.
I. Wygoda, Mark L., 1951–   .
II. Title.
DS135.P63W945    2003
940.53'18—dc21
97-21147

# CONTENTS

*Illustrations follow pages 26, 110, and 140*

# FOREWORD
## Michael Berenbaum

Imagine a Polish Jew, whose parents, siblings, and son have been murdered in the gas chambers of the Nazi death camps, commanding an Italian partisan unit. It would seem like a fantasy, a situation so strange that it could not have happened. Yet it did.

Oftentimes what happened in the Holocaust far exceeds our imagination. So it is with the evil and so, too, with the experience of the victim. As I listen to video testimonies or read memoirs, I am always struck by the unexpectedness of what happened.

If someone had told me the story of Hermann Wygoda, I might have dismissed it as excessive exaggeration or self-aggrandizement, the fanciful tale of a man who sought revenge in imagination for what was denied him in reality. And yet I would have been wrong. For Hermann Wygoda's experience in Italy is documented by independent sources, his honors confirmed by military records. His tales of exploits are understated, especially when read in the context of other memoirs by his Italian comrades in arms. Thus, his story is corroborated, and throughout the pages that follow, the reader will sense that his story rings true.

Wygoda is unusually dispassionate. There is little room for melancholy within this work, for moments of sentimentality. He is precise in his observations of himself and of others. He is unusually candid about the luck that led to his survival and keen in his understanding of the skills that permitted him to emerge. Early in his tale Wygoda writes that the clues to his survival are to be found in his physiology. "I was healthy and strong, and the challenge was fascinating." At thirty-three he was the appropriate age to survive.

As a rule, only the young and able-bodied could survive. Those who were too old could not endure the hunger, the conditions, or even the agony and uncertainty of the future; those who were too young, ill, or frail did not last long. We can understand Wygoda's self-characterization as healthy and strong, then, but how are we to understand his description of the challenge of survival as "fascinating?" It may give us the clue to Wygoda's strange journey.

Women with children were made vulnerable by their offspring, and fathers often felt bound to protect their families and could not wander from place to place. Wygoda's son, Samuel, is with his father from time to time, but Samuel is left with his uncle, Hermann's brother. Samuel is later placed in foster care with a friend, where his identity is concealed until his presence arouses too much curiosity and endangers the safety of his host family. He is then returned to the ghetto from which he is ultimately deported to death. Thus, Hermann is left alone, without encumbrances, but he is also alone emotionally. True, he has good friends who are loyal to him and to whom he is unfailingly loyal. They bond only for a time, however, and when that time passes, each is on his own. Few women appear in the narrative. There is too little time and too much danger for an interest in women.

An editorial footnote tells us that Hermann's memoirs do not deal with the death of his son. Wygoda shrouds that loss in silence. Perhaps it is too painful to confront. Perhaps he did not want the knowledge of those events to burden his new family, for whom the memoirs were translated. We learn that adjacent to Hermann's bed was a picture of Samuel. The first son was ever present, but his name was never spoken, his story never told. Are we to surmise that the absent one was always present, even in silence, especially in silence? Writing of his dead son might have pierced Hermann's armor of dispassion and thus paralyzed his efforts to remember and record.

Early on Wygoda learns what he perceives to be other essentials of survival. He had an acute sense of impending danger. He understood that he required the ability to hide fear and walk upright, as well as a willingness to lie about identity. His language skills served him well. Fluent in German as well as in other middle European languages, he understood what was happening, whether as a prisoner or when passing as a non-Jew. He could appear comfortable among his would-be tormentors. When necessary, he would ride in train cars reserved for Germans and dare them to uncover his true identity. Safety was often in proximity to the enemy.

There is a simple dignity to some of Wygoda's keenest judgments. Without any reflection, he says in passing that when the decree was issued forcing all Jews to register and to wear an arm band with the Star of David, he did not comply. "I was quite aware of the consequences, but I could not submit to such barbaric treatment and was determined to go underground if necessary." All too soon he had no choice but to move underground, roaming Poland with a false identity. Still, Wygoda sensed dangers early. Again, he says in passing that when anti-Jewish proclamations appeared regularly, he stopped reading them. Hermann was thus able to reduce his level of anxiety by removing himself from the constant discussion of impending doom. He thus kept his fear at an acceptable level. "Audacity is a prerequisite [for survival]," he writes. Then, in clinical terms reminiscent of the observations of Primo Levi, he demonstrates his audacity with great control and without accompanying drama.

Beginning students of the Holocaust often search for a formula of survival, a strategy that worked for all survivors, one that differentiated those who made it through from those who were killed. The deeper they delve into this evil, however, the more frustrating their search, because they fail to see a pattern in survival. Alas, there was none. The juxtaposition of chance, opportunity, and good fortune masks the skills that were required. And every survivor knows someone with greater skills, more strength, more cunning, more wisdom, and more daring who, by accident of circumstances, did not survive.

Wygoda articulates his own understanding of how to survive: "Unable to find a set rule to follow safely, I came to the inescapable conclusion that the only thing to do was to continue with my ad hoc improvisations." There could be no grand strategy, no established game plan, only a series of tactics to be applied as the situation required and modified on the spur of the moment. One had to be constantly on guard. One had to sense the danger and the opportunities and exploit whatever slim hopes presented themselves.

Still, we read of plans. Hermann and his companion Leon worked out a plan in the event of separation. Hermann constantly weighed alternatives.

There are few expressions of feeling in this book, not because Hermann was an unfeeling man, but rather because his feelings were repressed by the anxiety of the moment, by the discipline required for the struggle to survive. When life returned to quasi normality, albeit temporarily, concern for his family grew, anxiety over the fate of his son, brother, and mother intensified, but no such feelings were expressed in those times when he struggled to survive. Perhaps he intuitively understood that he could not afford such feelings if he were to survive the war. When the war ended and his struggle to survive was complete, Hermann noted his inability to feel, the emptiness at the core of his being. Not even loss: "I felt in a kind of vacuum. I was overcome by restlessness; nothing mattered to me." Only in peace could he confront the skeletons, face the void. He knew that it was easier to make decisions about other people's lives than to make them about his own.

Wygoda describes his wartime experience as "naked realism." His tone is true; his realism, abundant. He writes with gratitude of Stan, a non-Jewish friend who for a time offered his home as a haven and endangered his family for Samuel. One cannot write that the boy was sent into hiding; rather, he was required to live with a clandestine identity, a modern Marrano—he was Christian on the outside, but the mark of the covenant, the circumcision, could reveal his true identity at a moment's notice. Stan's "gesture," Wygoda writes, "was more than just noble. It was altruism at its fullest." Still, after a short time the offer of a haven became perilous to Stan's family. Neighbors are too curious. People begin to talk.

Hermann does not bemoan this change of fate that imperiled and ultimately proved lethal to his son. He understands that one must be grateful for the difficult. One has no right to expect the impossible. As we mystify the heroism of those who rescue, it would be wise to emphasize that most people found merely momentary havens; only a few found permanent havens that could withstand the pressures of changing circumstances or that endured even when the family was at risk. Many rescuers were generous within the limits of their humanity. More cannot be expected.

Wygoda's memoir offers some unusual information. He was an eyewitness to Treblinka, the death camp in which perhaps as many as 850,000 Jews were murdered. There are perhaps as few as nine known survivors. Thus, his recollections of the atmosphere surrounding the train station and the retelling of his conversations with local inhabitants who were eyewitnesses to the scene and who smelled the odor of burning flesh are particularly important. A generation later Claude Lanzmann would interview these bystanders for his memorable film *Shoah* and reveal how much they knew. He underscored how little they seemed to care.

Wygoda found safety for a time at the epicenter of the Third Reich. He lived in Berlin and used his linguistic skill and basic cunning to secure employment and promotion as a valuable employee successfully managing major business affairs. He was not the only Jew to find safety within the shadows of the Reichstag—nor was he the only Jew to have experienced the pleasure of seeing Allied bombs drop on Berlin. He knew full well that these bombs could kill him without notice, yet he understood that each bomb hastened the end of the war. Unlike Jakov Lind, who could not control himself as the Allied bombs descended and literally danced in the street, Wygoda was never out of control, never out of character. His inner self was hidden; his joy was deep but silent. His feelings were intense yet masked.

How does a Polish Jew become the commander of an Italian partisan unit? I will leave the details to Hermann's memoir—the escape to Italy, his arrest and escape, his contact with the partisans, and his desire for revenge. Hermann is sparing, far too sparing, with the details of his meteoric rise. He comments in passing that he was a compromise candidate among warring factions. The outsider was neither trusted nor distrusted by either side, and so when neither faction would yield, Hermann came to the fore. It is a complex narrative that must be accepted on faith. He does not reveal—perhaps because he is too modest to describe—the sturdiness of his presence that ultimately led others to accept his leadership. Nor does he write at length of the military exploits of an Italian partisan unit operating behind enemy lines in 1944, when Allied armies were advancing from the south and German armies had reinstated Mussolini in the north after his overthrow. There is little bravado—Wygoda is restrained in details of military operations and achievements.

Wygoda understood well the requirements of partisan warfare. Above all, the partisans required the support of the local population. The locals were the indispensable means to keep the partisans informed of enemy movements and thus provided the intelligence information necessary to inflict losses on the enemy and frustrate their plans. Left unsaid is that because of local support, partisan fighters were hidden during searches and could disappear among the populace without fears of betrayal. Wygoda does not deceive himself that the Italian partisan unit would have enjoyed the same measure of support a year earlier, in 1943, when the outcome of the war was still somewhat in doubt and when Germany could still inflict significant punishment on the local population.

By inference, we can understand why Jewish partisan activity in Poland was so difficult. Jews did not enjoy the support of the local populations. Because of differences in language and accents, as well as appearances, Jews could not easily mingle among the native population without fear of betrayal. Moreover, Jewish men were vulnerable because they alone of the Eastern European male populations were circumcised. For these reasons, resistance movements in Eastern Europe lacked even the most elementary conditions for successful partisan warfare.

Hermann, who used "Enrico" as his *nom de guerre,* mentions only in passing the other rules of partisan warfare. He writes, "It goes without saying that we could not afford to keep any prisoners." Thus, captured enemy soldiers were killed as a matter of course. He silences his conscience with regards to his wartime behavior, not by speaking of the evils of the enemy, but by invoking his code of conduct, the ethical norms that guided the most unethical of warfare: "I did not kill indiscriminately. I never tortured anyone."

As a partisan leader, Wygoda encountered German fighting forces on a more personal and far more equal basis than he would have as one of their nameless and faceless Jewish victims. Enrico met one prisoner in particular, an officer so methodical as to write the dates and locations of executions, retaining photographs as proof of his achievements. The German officer justified his deeds. "Justice, he said . . . , had to be done to the bandits who were disturbing the peaceful life of the communities of which he had been in charge." The officer begged Hermann to have pity on his three little children and wife. Hermann comments that the lieutenant's action sent a "feeling of sickening disgust" through him. He turned away and gave the order "to follow the usual procedure in cases where Nazis were involved."

Wygoda concludes without hatred, seemingly without rancor. "In my opinion, the Nazis were not entitled to any benefit derived from international law or any other custom practiced by civilized people anywhere in the world." This conclusion of a fighter is little different from the philosophical conclusion of Martin Buber, who felt that since the Nazis had abandoned the norms of common humanity, it was impossible to behave toward them within those norms.

Wygoda assumes that his readers are generally informed about the Holocaust, that his story can be seen in the much larger context of the events of the time. Perhaps this introduction can offer less well informed readers the background they need to understand his singular story.

✡

In Poland the onset of the Holocaust began in earnest on September 1, 1939, the date of the German invasion of Poland. In the month before the invasion, the foreign ministers of Germany and the Soviet Union signed a secret agreement dividing Poland in two. Germany would invade from the west, the Soviet Union would enter in the east, and the country would be divided into spheres of influence. For Jews the invasion marked the onset of lethal danger. Choices were to be made. Does one remain in the city or flee to the countryside? Does one flee to Soviet-held territory or remain in German-occupied Poland? For more than a century, safety had been in the West. That lesson had to be unlearned.

In German-occupied Poland the war against the Jews proceeded from persecution to ghettoization and then, following the decision to kill all Jews and the creation of the apparatus for their destruction—the six killing centers—in late spring and early summer 1942, to deportation to death camps.

Still, although the pattern seems clear in retrospect, the move from persecution to ghettoization and ultimately to murder could not have been anticipated. Historians still debate how improvised these plans were. Suffice it to say that Jews who lived through these events, as Hermann Wygoda did, could not know in advance where they would lead. Each step came as a surprise; each called forth a different tactic for survival. Let me stress the word *tactic,* for as Wygoda so correctly notes, there could be no long-term strategy, merely a series of improvised moves.

Wygoda chose to survive alone, not in community, not among Jews, but as a Marrano, assuming a series of false identities, improvising his plans, sensing immediate danger and constantly on the run. He was constantly on the run while the Jews were persecuted. He was constantly on the run while the Jews of Poland were ghettoized. He traveled from ghetto to ghetto, entering those holding pens of Jews and then leaving to seek safety elsewhere. He was constantly on the run while Jews were being deported to their deaths. His tactics were individual. One person could find a temporary haven, but a community could not simply disappear.

Safety is often found in the eye of the storm. Thus, Wygoda went to Germany from Poland, for there was a shortage of labor in Germany. His language skills helped him. His business acumen was quickly exploited by his bosses. He found safety as a representative of the Germans in occupied territories, among those who boasted that they could smell the Jew, that they could sense the Jew on contact. With Germany becoming a place of danger and his own situation growing ever more untenable, he escaped to Italy—an Italy that, in 1944, was quite different from the Italy of the war's early years.

Although Jews came to Italy even before the Roman conquest of Judea and the destruction of Jerusalem in 70 C.E., Jews constituted only 0.1 percent of the Italian population in the twentieth century. Even as non-Catholics, they were full participants in Italian culture and society, prominent in professional and intellectual life.

Fascist Italy ruled by Benito Mussolini was an ally of Hitler's Germany. During Mussolini's rule, however, no Jews were deported from Italy or from Italian-controlled territories. In fact, Jews were better treated in Fascist Italian-occupied parts of France than they were in Vichy France. The fateful year in Italy was 1943. Allied armies had invaded the South, Mussolini was overthrown, and a separate peace was signed. Germany invaded and occupied Italy, reinstated Mussolini, and began deporting Italian Jews.

Previous anti-Jewish Italian laws were a pale imitation of German racial law, and Italians were less than diligent about enforcing them. The Italians found it difficult to discriminate systematically against Jews on the basis of blood; the Italian government was unwilling to provoke the Roman Catholic church, which spoke out on behalf of those who had converted. (The pope saw fit to protest the racial laws only as they affected Jews who had converted to Catholicism.)

The Italians were generally undisciplined about inquiring into Jewish origins. Bribery was routine, and official documents were easily concocted.

Susan Zuccotti, a historian of Italy and the Holocaust, writes that through these venal practices, the Italians seemed to be "honoring the most corrupt and penalizing, by default, the most worthy (those who refused to lie about their backgrounds)." Zuccotti believes that under the pressure of war, "the Italian tendency in routine times to ignore the law" became "a determination to evade it."

The roundups of Jews in Italy began only in the spring on 1943, a year after the deportations from Poland, two full years after the murder of Jews began in the invaded territories of the Soviet Union. They continued throughout the fall and winter of 1943–44. Despite these efforts, eight out of ten Jews escaped capture. Of the 40,000 Jews in Italy, 8,000 were killed.

✡

Why were Italian Jews saved in large numbers? The deportation of Jews began late, when Germany's defeat seemed inevitable. In Poland the Nazis had five years to do their work; in the Netherlands, four. In Italy only a year elapsed between the onset of deportation and liberation by the Allies.

It was during this final year, when the outcome of the war could no longer be in doubt, that Wygoda escaped to Italy. He worked in the north, behind enemy lines, in an area where partisans were engaged in effective action against the Germans. The landscape was helpful—the mountain terrain offered broad views and narrow paths. Soviet partisans found safety in the forests. Italian partisans found a place of refuge in the mountains.

The men Hermann commanded were treated well by the civilian populations, who intuitively understood that the future was on their side. The desire to collaborate with the Germans had diminished, the fear of the Germans had lessened, and the situation of the Italian partisans had thus significantly eased even before Wygoda entered. This permitted his operation to enjoy freedom of movement. He was probably chosen to lead because he was an outsider and thus less caught up in the battle for the future and more engrossed in the campaign against the Germans.

The seemingly imaginative, fanciful story of living "in the shadow of the swastika" proves true. Both the substance and the style of the narrative add to the texture of our understanding of the Holocaust and of the responses of Jews of diverse ages, experiences, and temperaments to the assault on their very being. Hermann Wygoda survived alone. His choices were singular, and his experiences were unique. The more we delve into this history, the more we understand that the power of the Holocaust is intensified by our learning of each narrative, each individual tale.

# ACKNOWLEDGMENTS

While attending the dedication of the United States Holocaust Memorial Museum with my sisters on April 22, 1993, I decided to prepare for publication the memoirs that our father had begun while living in a cave in northern Italy nearly fifty years in the past. Twenty years later he translated his Polish words into English for his children, so that one day we would know the history of his years during the war, a history of which he rarely spoke. As I sat in the cold rain with thousands of others and listened to the music and the prayers and the speeches, my thoughts were of my father. I decided that a fitting tribute to him, now long overdue, would be for the world—not just his children—to know what he had accomplished in Nazi-occupied Europe, and that I, rather than someone who never knew him, should be the one to put his memoirs into final form for publication.

I am deeply indebted to several individuals who aided me in the preparation of this book. My sisters, Sylvia Wygoda and Lois Wygoda Klezmer, helped and encouraged me throughout the project. I am especially grateful to my niece Deborah Klezmer, who wrote the introduction to this book and provided me with substantial editorial assistance. Paul Peregal, with whom I had not had contact since we met briefly at the 1967 World's Fair in Montreal, provided me with photographs and copies of his father's written and oral histories and wrote this book's memorial for Leon Peregal. I am happy that a friendship has developed between us as a result of this project.

I thank Gray Little for his highly skilled technical assistance with the photographs and documents, all of which are from our family's personal collection, except where noted otherwise.

Special thanks go to my editor Judith McCulloh, whose insight, inspiration, and passion for this project guided me at every stage and touched this book in myriad ways. Thanks also to manuscript editor Bruce Bethell for his attention to detail and respect for my father's voice. It has been a pleasure bringing this book into the world with both of them.

I also would like to acknowledge Tom Fox, Bruno Borsari, Joe Magedanz, and Siegi Izakson for help with translations and Maurice Gold, Cheryl Ware, Paul Peregal, Bonny Fetterman, Alex De Grand, and Michael Berenbaum for reading the manuscript and offering their most helpful suggestions.

M.W.

# INTRODUCTION
## Deborah Klezmer

After Hermann Wygoda died, I requested only one of his possessions, his cap. I wore his white cap, which snapped in the front, for weeks after his death. The cap smelled like Hermann. It smelled of dusty books, of soil, of cement. It smelled of family and music. But above all else, it smelled to me of the sea and the live shrimp Hermann placed in my right hand as he placed a hook in the left. The Hermann I knew was a fisherman. On sun-streaked days we walked together to the dock behind his house, dropped our lines, and waited in silence. Hermann was a man of many silences.

It is the picture of Hermann's white cap, shielding his eyes from the sun, that has withstood the pull of time against memory. When Hermann was alive, I was still very young, too young to know that the man with whom I fished on weekends every summer was a traveler of the world. As I became a bit older, though, I learned about Europe and the Holocaust. Like most Jewish children, I was shown piles of shoes, eyeglasses, watches, and human hair, as well as other images that have continued to haunt me well into my adult life. By the time I entered fourth grade, already I knew the word *survivor*.

Hermann, I knew, was a survivor.

Hermann Wygoda was born in Offenbach, Germany, on November 18, 1906, the eldest of Maier and Chana Wygoda's two sons. He and his younger brother, Leon, were raised in the traditions of Judaism. Chana saw to it that her sons acquired her native Polish language, and the summers that the boys spent in her hometown of Kossow with her blacksmith father, Samuel, ensured their fluency in both Polish and German. After Maier was killed in

World War I, Chana was left to raise her boys alone. Eventually the family moved to Kossow, where Chana took work as a professional matchmaker and Leon made a living in cabinetmaking. Hermann obtained an engineering degree from Warsaw Polytechnic Institute, served as a lieutenant in the Polish Army, and worked as a civil engineer specializing in the construction of bridges. He moved to Berlin, the most vital city for the European intelligentsia of the 1920s, where he worked in industry until 1929. Hermann then returned to Poland, a country in which three million Jews would soon be annihilated. He married a woman whose name is now unknown, and in 1934, before separating, they had a son, Samuel. While Hermann remained in Warsaw, his young son went to live in Kossow with Chana and Leon. Hermann's memoirs begin on September 1, 1939, when the Nazis invaded Poland. With this first day of bombing and terror, World War II began. En route to Poland, trains carrying German soldiers bore the slogan "We're going to Poland to beat up the Jews."

Unlike many Jews who were forced into hiding, Hermann moved with relative ease through the early years of the war by successfully masking his Jewish identity and posing as an ethnic German. His physical appearance, fluency in German, and bold nature saved his life several times on any given day. His travels during the war took him from Poland to Estonia, Finland, and Germany, before he escaped from an Italian prison and headed into the mountains of northern Italy. From a solitary life in a cave, he became "Enrico," the leader of a large partisan division fighting against the Nazis and the Fascists; he did this despite his nationality and religion, which differed from those of the hundreds of men and women under his command. He interrogated captured Nazis, ordered their executions, and engaged in face-to-face negotiations with a Nazi commander over the exchange of prisoners. During these years Hermann began to note his wartime experiences in a journal that, had it been found on his person by the enemy, easily might have cost him his life; this journal would later provide the basis for his memoirs. After he and his fellow partisans liberated the Italian city of Savona, he received decorations from three western powers, including the U.S. Army's Bronze Star.

Although Hermann's manuscript covers this seven-year period extensively, there are key details that apparently he never spoke of or recorded. He begins his manuscript by writing about his mother, his brother, and his son, all of whom then vanish from his narrative, leaving behind barely a trace of memory. We do not know when or how Hermann learned of their deaths; in fact, he nowhere notes their deaths in Treblinka during 1942. We know nothing of the circumstances immediately preceding their deaths. Because of the lack of such crucial details, Hermann's memoirs tell an incredible story, not just of World War II or one Jew's passion for survival, but also of memory, of how we bury the dead within ourselves as if we could protect them from the world. We will find Hermann's mother, brother, and son as we read, for they are always there, on every page, in the silence.

Following the war, receipt of the Bronze Star in 1946 facilitated approval of Hermann's application to immigrate to the United States. He crossed the Atlantic on the *Ile-de-France*, which sailed from Cherbourg. He writes: "The term *death*, which has been referred to as 'Majesty,' lost every meaning for me, except when I was capable of applying it in conjunction with the term *Nazi*. Then, and only then, did death have a meaning for me, inasmuch as it helped to carry out an act of justice against the killers of innocent children. At times such thoughts frightened me. I wondered what it would be like after all this came to an end, when I again would be a free man in a peaceful world."

On November 20, 1946, Hermann arrived in New York to begin a new life. He made his way to the home of his mother's sister, his Aunt Ella, in Chattanooga, Tennessee. There he met Rae Raider, who had a five-year-old daughter, Lois. Hermann and Rae were married in May 1947, and Hermann adopted Lois. Together the couple briefly owned and operated a small grocery store while Hermann laid the groundwork for what was to become a successful home-building business, the Wygoda Building Corporation. Today hundreds of families in Chattanooga live in homes designed, built, and sold by Hermann in the fifties and sixties. A second daughter, Sylvia, was born in 1948, and a son, Mark, followed in 1951. Hermann built the family home on Glendon Drive, as well as a cottage on Lake Chickamauga, where he also built a dock so that he could fish anytime at all.

Every night the family ate dinner together, on Fridays Hermann accompanied his wife and children to temple, and on Passover he made gefilte fish from his own fresh catch. He never told his children how he had been shot in the leg, and respectful of his silence his children never asked. After sundown he listened to his shortwave radio and monitored events in Europe. He slept with two pictures on his nightstand: that of a young girl to whom he had smuggled food until her death in the Warsaw Ghetto, and that of his son, Samuel. Miraculously Hermann had carried these pictures on his person during the entire war. Sometimes he slept through the night; other times, unable to withstand the sound of gunfire, he got out of bed to silence the occasional war movie enjoyed by his uncomprehending children.

Extremely patriotic, Hermann regularly packed his family into the station wagon and took off on long drives for all-American sights, such as Mount Rushmore and the White House. His children had seen most of the country by the time they headed for college. Concerned about national defense, he joined the civil defense during the cold war, which gave him permission to carry his gun in case of emergency.

While his children were in school, Hermann attended temple regularly for Sabbath services. He observed the high holidays there, and the family attended temple events, going each year for the seder on the second night of Passover. Clearly, though, there were aspects of his religion with which he had question. Each year on the first night of Passover, as he conducted his family's seder, he would stop reading from time to time, shake his head, and mumble quietly, "This is ridiculous." Despite his ties to the temple and his commitment to bringing up his children in the traditions in which he had been raised, I cannot help but wonder if he believed in God. It is a question among many others that I would have liked to ask him. For Hermann, I think, religion meant family, and family meant God.

In 1966, no longer able to bear the call of memory in silence, Hermann took up his fountain pen and in green ink began translating from Polish into English the journal he had kept in the mountains. *In the Shadow of the Swastika* is the result of his efforts. This was a recounting, he said, meant for his children, so that they would know what had happened to him and his family during the war. His primary intent for writing was not publication; indeed, he seems to have had varied opinions as to whether such accounts could act as long-lasting truths in the world. He writes: "Many books have already been written about this epochal event in our lifetime, and much more literature will be written on the subject for many years to come. All of it will finally be lost in the labyrinth of legends, and then fable, in not too many generations hence." Still, he took the countless hours necessary to record his days battling the Nazis and Fascists, as if harboring a subtle faith in the consequence of sharing such experiences. There will come a day, in our lifetime, when there will be no survivors left to bear witness for us, and it will be up to us to teach our children what happened to the great-grandparents whom they have never known. As we struggle to explain, I believe it will be Hermann's memoirs, and the memoirs of other survivors, that will give our children more of the truth.

In grade school, as I absorbed the landscape shown to me in films, pictures, and books about the Holocaust, I saw Jews lined up against concrete walls, packed onto trains, and huddled together in showers; never once in four years of study was I shown a single Jew who took up arms against the Nazis. Whereas Hermann worried that the passage of time and the proliferation of stories would dilute history, it seems that now—five decades since the end of the war—as the stories of Jewish resistance leaders are finally beginning to emerge, it is this very proliferation of detail that will challenge us to pursue as much truth as can be found. We should not have been kept so long from our heroes.

In 1972 Hermann and Rae moved to Cape Coral, Florida, only a couple of hours' drive from my family's house. On weekends we went to their home to eat bagels and sit by the pool. Later, a voracious reader, I was stretched out on the lawn chair reading the Judy Blume book *Are You There, God? It's Me, Margaret* when Hermann asked to see what I was reading. I handed him the book, which he looked at for a minute, turning it over to read the back cover. Still reading, he walked off the porch. When Hermann returned, he gave me an orange-and-black hardcover book. It was *The Will to Doubt*, by Bertrand Russell. I was nine years old.

As I write tonight on Yom Kippur, the light of the *Yahrzeit* candle throws shadows on the bookshelves. I am at home here, among my scattered papers and books. They remind me of childhood afternoons passed spying in Hermann's office, inching titles from their rows and standing perplexed, slightly excited, as I peered at words in Polish, German, Italian, French, Latin, Spanish, Russian, and English. I sat in Hermann's massive green leather chair and stared at his desk set (with letter opener, magnifying glass, and penholder), inhaling the sweet, dusty smell of manuscripts in their senior years. Protected by walls of books, I dreamed I was a writer, like Hermann.

Judaism teaches us that people live on in the acts of goodness they perform and in the hearts and minds of those who love them. Just as Hermann later knew the necessity of revisiting his own experiences during the war to keep meaning alive, so too must we commit ourselves to revisiting the lives and deaths of the more than twelve million men, women, and children who were tortured and murdered when Hitler and his SS men rode the crest of evil, flooding Europe with blood. How could we live with ourselves knowing that, though our ancestors gave their lives, we had failed in our comparatively minor task of keeping them alive in our memory? How can we live with ourselves if we do not honor their lives and deaths by taking every possible measure to ensure that future generations recognize the rising stench of hatred?

We live in an age of murderers. For more than three years we watched pictures of "ethnic cleansing" in Bosnia-Herzegovina flicker across our televisions. These images of mass rape, murder, shelling, famine, disease, malnutrition, and a generation of lost children are replicated every day in our own country as women are tortured and murdered by their spouses; gunfire rings out in our streets, schools, temples, mosques, and churches; the homeless freeze to death on filthy sidewalks; and children grow up thinking that brutality is an ordinary way of life. Today our family brings Hermann's memoirs out of the privacy of our home and offers them to the public with hopes of inspiring the best in us to fight for our own rights and lives, as well as for the rights and lives of people whom we have never met and will never meet. Hermann Wygoda, and those who fought beside him in the Fourth Brigade, are proof that a difference can be made by everyday men and women. Even in cultures bankrupted by violence and fear, there are always heroes who make us want to better the world for our children, as Hermann bettered the world for his children and his children's children. I know, because Hermann was my grandfather.

In 1982, when I was fifteen, my mother, Lois, took me to the hospital to see Hermann. Suffering from refractory anemia, he slipped in and out of silence, searching for the loved ones he'd lost and drawing closer to another, soundless world. From time to time the coma broke and he opened his eyes, slowly. There were moments when he spoke to us, but often we did not understand what he was saying. He was in no pain, and there was no chance for recovery. All we could do was be present with him so he would not be frightened or alone as he prepared to die. I remember in particular a long day of waiting in which my uncle Mark took me by the hand and led me outside the hospital. We sat beside each other on a cement bench, he with his arm around my shoulders. We cried together. To this day, I believe it was Mark's willingness to share his emotion that helped me navigate this, my first experience with death.

After Mark and I had returned to the room, Hermann mumbled something we could not understand. Eyes closed, determined, he tried again. He said the word *Kaddish*. Although Kaddish, known as the Mourner's Prayer, is said only after a person has died, we assumed that Hermann wanted us to say Kaddish for him, perhaps because he wanted to hear it when he was alive, perhaps because he thought he had already died. As I was the only one with a reading knowledge of Hebrew, my aunt Sylvia handed me a prayerbook.

The family stood around the bed while I read aloud. In the thirteen years since Hermann's death, I have taken it for granted that, because he was dying, the prayer was meant for him. As I recently studied his memoirs, however, this explanation began to feel inadequate. Tonight, as the *Yahrzeit* candle burns to its end, I believe he wanted to say Kaddish himself for Chana, Leon, and Samuel Wygoda, as well as for all those who could not escape the Nazis. Too tired and weak to say the words, a few days before his death he said the prayer one last time, forced to settle for his granddaughter's timid voice. On May 18, 1982, Hermann took his place among his mother, brother, son and all else that has survived the war, so much of which is silence. Three days later he was laid to rest in the Mizpah Congregation cemetery in Chattanooga, Tennessee.

Strung like thread through my childhood is the echo of one question: why didn't they resist? It is hard for me to admit that as a child I was both embarrassed and ashamed to be among a people who, I was told, were passive, weak. Not until now, nearly age thirty, have I learned the truth. Hermann's story has taught me that some Jews did take up arms against the Nazis; it has also taught me, however, that a victim does not have to bear arms to resist. In my mind it is Hermann himself, not his recounting of the Holocaust, that is in danger of turning to legend. If in explaining his strength we think of him as more than a man, we separate him from us as being better or stronger than other men. This both explains his extraordinary actions and releases us of any obligation to act with comparable courage. Hermann was a hero, but so too was he a man. Even in the cruelest hours of war, Jews all over Europe resisted; they resisted by surviving another hour, another day. Each moment they lived through was a moment of courage, of honor, of resistance.

On summer days when the sun is high I see him still, towering over me as his strong arm and wrist gracefully demonstrate the perfect cast. Then he takes off his cap and puts it on my small head. As I look up at him, watching the slight smile play at his lips, I ask if he believes in God. Instead of answering, he widens his smile, and I know that Hermann has caught me a fish.

In the Shadow of the Swastika

# Prologue

In 1966, while convalescing from a major illness, I decided to translate my memoirs, which I had written in Polish during the war, into English to acquaint my children with the often tragic experiences that I survived. With plenty of legal pads, I started. It took me some ninety days to complete seven years of my life's history.

It first came to me in December 1944 to write down what was happening. That was the time of year when the usually heavy snowfall began in the Ligurian Mountains, otherwise known as the Maritime Alps. The following month the normal accumulation of snow reached approximately five feet in depth throughout the area of my activity. Circulation under such conditions was highly impaired for both the partisans and for the enemy. Nonetheless, the war had to go on, if not by direct contact, then by other means, including the nightly exchange of artillery and mortar fire between us and the Fascist San Marco Division. Additionally, our reconnaissance elements were well equipped and trained in the use of snow shoes as well as skis so that they could continue their activities.

But the heavy accumulation of snow, which naturally restricted my movements, turned out to be beneficial, since it redirected my attention to something very important: reliving my experiences. The crystal-clear mountain air, the pure white snow, the diamond-like multicolored frozen particles reflecting the sun, and the calm serenity of the environment inspired me to write down those events that were continuously on my mind, starting several years back with my experiences that had begun on September 1, 1939.

While writing, memory posed no obstacle. All those experiences were still fresh in my mind. Even today, so many years later, most of those tragic days in my life stay before me clearly as though they happened only yesterday.

After the war I decided to immigrate to the United States of America to find peace of mind and tranquility, which I found in abundance. I also reunited with a younger sister of my late mother who had immigrated to the United States before the war. My life in this wonderful country has been very good in every possible respect.

Contemporary map of Europe showing the locations of several cities to which the author refers in his memoirs.

# PART 1
# Poland

# 1    First Days of the War

I awoke suddenly to the combined shrills of the air-defense system and the thundering explosions of antiaircraft guns. It was around four o'clock in the morning on September 1, 1939. I was living in an apartment building in the Praga suburb of Warsaw on the day of the invasion.

The first targets of the Nazi Stukas early that morning were the four railroad stations in metropolitan Warsaw, two of which were located in Praga. All four stations were in such densely populated sections that the first bombs dropped on Warsaw killed scores of innocent civilians and injured hundreds more.

In their first air raid the Nazis also destroyed the municipal airport and silenced Radio Warsaw, which at the time was one of the major radio stations in Europe. Of course another well-known station was still on the air. Radio Gleiwitz, the major Hitlerite propaganda instrument in that part of Europe before and during the war, broadcast nothing but military marching tunes throughout the morning. Then the music stopped as an announcer read, in Hitler's name, a special proclamation from the Deutsche Welle in Berlin: "In order to defend the German Reich from a flagrant aggression committed by its neighbor Poland, the führer and commander-in-chief of the armed forces of the fatherland has ordered the German armed forces to counterattack and cross the German-Polish border in pursuit of the invader."

The announcement of Hitler's proclamation to the German people came several hours after the beginning of the bombardment, and only a few civilians who possessed a shortwave radio and understood the German language (as I did) knew then what had happened. Because Radio Warsaw was out of commission, most people found out hours later when the news finally reached them by word of mouth.

Many residents immediately began trying to leave the city, believing that they would have a better chance to survive in the open countryside. Going anywhere by train was impossible because the city's entire transportation system was paralyzed that first day. As a result, the roads and highways leading out of Warsaw were jammed with refugees fleeing the city. Nazi fliers discovered that these crowded avenues of escape gave them a perfect opportunity to engage in mass slaughter without running the risk of being shot down. News of the killing spread quickly, and the exodus ended.

Transportation outage was only one of the many immediate problems created by the bombardment. Food shortage was another. Most stores never opened their doors that first day. In those days very few people in Warsaw had any facility for food storage; refrigerators were still considered a luxury, and the public was accustomed to buying their food supply fresh daily. Later in the afternoon, as the bombings decreased, some of the stores did open but kept their most sought-after items off the shelves. These items were obtainable, however, for the proper price. Those who were able to make these under-the-counter purchases had to be let out of the store through the back door.

The afternoon calm was of short duration. The Nazis' shrieking Stukas were soon back in full force over the city, this time concentrating on the two railroad stations that were least damaged in the earlier attack, as well as on a nearby warehouse. Wanton destruction continued intermittently throughout the day. In addition to trying to avoid being killed by the falling bombs, the city's residents had to help others who were already hurt and watch out in case the buildings in which they were living went up in flames. It was a hectic day indeed.

Warsaw's communication system remained in disarray during the first week of bombing. Attempts to make a long-distance telephone call were dangerous because suspicion was rampant. The hysteria generated by the bombings and the accompanying suspicion caused many innocent people to lose their lives. To be seen looking out a window during a bombing raid was sufficient reason to be killed immediately, and only those who were lucky enough to have someone nearby to help identify them were saved from being shot. Asking for the location of a street or for general directions was dangerous. Those who were so unfortunate as to be arrested for allegedly spying for the enemy or for directing Nazi fliers to their targets did not have the slightest chance to talk themselves out of their predicament. There was neither judge nor jury to help them.

Naturally, the intensification of the bombing produced a proportionate increase in the numbers of dead and wounded. The municipal hospital in my suburb was already heavily damaged from the first day of bombardment, so its capacity to treat the wounded was severely limited. Other city hospitals were overflowing with the injured. Although they no doubt could have been saved had treatment centers been available, many of the wounded died.

Mobilization as such never got under way because of the lack of transportation, and mobilization law was unenforceable without it. Only the forces existing at the time of attack were able to offer resistance to the invader. There was no shortage of men willing to fight for their country, however. In addition to the reserve units, whose report to duty was required by regulation, there were large numbers of men who volunteered for service. These were put together into units without regard to their specialties and were sent off on their own.

The elimination of almost the entire Polish Air Force on the first day of the war further complicated the defense problem. This left largely old artillery and machine guns as the only defense available. There were even instances when soldiers fired at the attacking planes with their 1918 French-made rifles. Rarely did I see a modern, rapid-firing machine gun in use. When available, however, machine guns were particularly effective in the defense of bridges, where they forced the enemy fliers to maneuver continuously to avoid getting hit, causing them to drop their bombs in the middle of the river rather than on the bridge.

On September 7, six days after the first bombing, Colonel Umiastowski, the commander of the city, issued an order for the male population of Warsaw to evacuate the city immediately. The evacuation was to take place as follows: the first to leave were to be the police force, second the military, and finally the unarmed civilians. All the government leaders had already abandoned the capital several days before, using the then quite scarce motor vehicles to carry them and their personal belongings to Romania.

It was indeed depressing to see the obese General Wladislaw Skladkowski, minister of the interior, and his redheaded French mistress leave the city ahead of a large, loaded personal convoy. He left in a hurry at night, using proper military strategy to save his neck, his purse, and his woman. This was the same general who had instigated the famous pogroms against the Jewish peddlers in the area of Chenstochowa during the midthirties. To pacify the landless peasants who were pushing for land reform in Chenstochowa, General Skladkowski directed their attention instead to the so-called prosperous Jews, who were barely making ends meet by operating little shops and stores in small towns and villages. Given the green light by the general, the peasants fell on their frightened victims, robbing, killing, and destroying most of what those poor people called their own, while the general's police looked the other way. Afterward, in a speech before the Sejm (Polish Parliament), the general called that pogrom "peaceful competition."

On the eighth day of the war, the city streets began filling with retreating soldiers and civilian refugees from the western part of the country. By the following day, chaos reigned; instead of organized military units making an orderly retreat, small groups of soldiers from what once was a proud Polish army frantically pushed their way through the civilian masses.

The tenth day of the war was marked by the first uninterrupted bombing of the city. From the early morning hours until dark, Nazi planes pounded Warsaw with bombs of various types and sizes, this time without the pretense that they were trying to destroy only military targets. Such indiscriminate destruction was intended to force the city to surrender. The devastation was terrible. Utilities were put completely out of order, and from that day forward water had to be carried by bucket from the Vistula River. Lack of cooking fuel was not a problem, however, for the general destruction left plenty of wood available. Lack of food was a problem, of course, but not an insurmountable one. There were dead horses all over town, and the cool nights and moderate days delayed their decomposition. Any objections one could have had to eating horse meat under normal conditions were not expressed in those all-but-normal times.

That day also brought another new, but not unexpected, element of misery: heavy artillery shelling began as soon as the city was surrounded. Human endurance can be tested under duress only, and there was no better testing ground than the Warsaw of September 1939. But the city was not yet ready to surrender, despite all the terror to which the population had been subjected. Those who would have surrendered—the ruling elite—had fled to Romania long before the avenues of escape had been closed.

We soon learned how to live under siege. Despite the day-and-night harassment by the enemy, we managed to get a few hours of sleep each day by stuffing our ears with cotton. We became accustomed to the companionship of exploding artillery shells. We could even tell from the sound of an incoming shell where it would fall and explode. We watched the planes break away from their formation and circle to drop a bomb. We then estimated its point of impact and quickly adjusted our position accordingly. It was like a cat-and-mouse game, where a mistake in judgment could mean death.

Some people on our block engaged in animated discussions regarding the situation at hand. These were rather spirited conversations with strong opinions being heatedly exchanged. At times an argument would escalate until even the worst bombardment would not stop it, unless perhaps a direct hit put an end to further debate.

The bombing now continued around the clock. Since the start of the war, the Nazis had tried to destroy the first bridge ever built in the city, the middle bridge on the Vistula River, which connected my suburb of Praga to the center of the city. They never succeeded in destroying that old bridge, however, despite the sparse defenses around it. They did manage to knock a hole here and there in the steel floor and damage the streetcar tracks, but the bridge still remained passable. In their attacks on the bridge, however, the Nazis succeeded in completely destroying a hospital located several blocks away, as well as a nearby church.

The news of the Soviet Union's march across the eastern border of Poland reached the city on September 18, although the invasion actually began the day before. That event generated less argument than one would have expected, considering its importance. This lack of concern was quite possibly due to the great physical and mental exhaustion already experienced, the losses already sustained, and the terror to which the people had already been subjected. Still, it did stimulate some interesting discussions at times when the bombing receded.

It was no secret that defeat was just around the corner. The only questions were how many more days the agony would last, and, when it was all over, who would occupy the city. With no electricity and very few battery-powered radios, we had to depend on gossip for our news. Since the intervention by the Russians, the gossip had indicated the demarcation line would be along the former Czarist-German border. The Vistula River was also mentioned. Ranked third as a possibility was the Bug River.

The only ones who took part in such discussions were the liberals or the politically independent. The other groups, such as the nationalists or the communists, took almost no part. Communists did not express themselves because they did not officially exist. Carrying on a clandestine existence for so many years made the communists cautious and distrustful of anyone they did not personally know. Thus it was impossible to get their opinion on such a delicate subject as the occupation of Warsaw. Likewise, the nationalists were understandably silent on the issue, but for a different reason.

During the heyday of collaboration between the Nazis and the Polish regime, General Skladkowski's dreaded Greenshirts had controlled the streets and had spread terror throughout the Jewish population. Modeled after those of the German Brownshirts, their uniforms consisted of the same style boots, caps, trousers, and so on and bore all the Nazi paraphernalia, including the twisted cross. After the start of the war, however, the Greenshirts found it more prudent to be less conspicuous. Now they were experiencing a terror that for them would have been unimaginable only a few short weeks before, when they had thought that they were the only ones entitled to subject others to terror.

The nationalists began to realize that all their boastful propaganda was indeed nothing more than propaganda. Their loud demands in the recent past for colonies in Angola, for a piece of territory in Czechoslovakia, or for a bit of Lithuania, which they believed they would get by following the führer in this conquest of Europe, now echoed in a strange way.

With both the communists and the nationalists silent, only the moderate elements could be heard speculating as to who would occupy the city, for occupation was a foregone conclusion. Everyone knew, or at least thought they knew, what to expect from the Nazis, but the Russians provided almost a complete mystery. Hatred and distrust had existed between Russians and Poles for centuries, and for the previous twenty years the Polish-Russian border had been the most tightly controlled in the world. Along the entire length of the common border, the Polish authorities observed the famous Cordon Sanitaire idea to the point of absurdity. This most recent period of animosity began at the end of World War I with the Russians' refusal to surrender some of their territory to the greedy Polish generals.

Although both invaders were almost equally hated, there was more concern about the Nazis than about the Russians. The more immediate problem, however, was how to stay alive. We had been living, or rather existing, under such miserable conditions that time slowed to a standstill. We could see no end to the suffering. Then, suddenly, the bombing and artillery barrage stopped. Rumors spread quickly throughout the city that an armistice had been signed, and people flocked into the streets in great masses to hunt for food and news.

During the four days between the apparent cease-fire and the Nazis' entry into the city, no food could be found. Nonetheless, some people knew that there were large military storage barracks in Praga where the defense ministry had stocked clothing and food. These warehouses had been full when the war began, and because the entire state rail network had been destroyed, nothing had been shipped to the front. Several who argued that the food rightfully belonged to Warsaw citizens were shot and killed by the Polish guards who remained on duty. Their foolish decision to protect the warehouses not only caused the deaths of compatriots but also saved the warehouses for the Nazis, who would find them full of supplies when they finally marched into the city.

In one other place, however, the Germans were not so lucky. Since Warsaw was a large industrial center, barges loaded with industrial supplies could always be found moored on the Vistula River. Some of these barges had been hit and sunk during the Nazis' attempt to destroy the bridges, but others were still afloat. During the four days prior to German occupation, hundreds of people swarmed over these barges and carried away everything that was not solidly fastened down. These materials included zinc blocks, bales of natural rubber, and aluminum sheets, as well as copper, stainless steel, leather, and raw materials for the soap and other industries. What they could not take, or did not have time to take, they set afire.

Except for the looting of these barges, quiet had prevailed during the cease-fire. Now and then a single German car would drive through the streets at high speed, and there was constant aerial surveillance. After the first of October, however, a large mass of men and equipment began to roll through Praga going north and east at a slow pace. At times I observed some of the younger soldiers attempting to fraternize with the population, but such attempts generally were not reciprocated.

Occupation by the Germans was something new only to the young. Barely twenty-one years had passed since the last German occupation, that time by the forces of Kaiser Wilhelm, and only twenty-three years earlier the Czarist Russians were driven out after their long occupation of the country. The current occupation was thus less shocking for the majority of the population than for the younger generation, which had grown up during the period of independence. Still, those who had experienced World War I knew the difference between the führer and the kaiser, and their fear and anxiety were correspondingly great.

The first train to arrive carried elements of the Wehrmacht, the German armed forces, who were entering Warsaw for the victory parade to be given for Adolf Hitler. Their expressions were rather happy, for they believed that it was the beginning of the victorious era in the thousand-year Reich, as had been predicted by their führer. In their wake came the SS. I was familiar with the Brownshirts from the time when I had lived in Berlin, but the SS had not then been organized. Thus, I had no basis on which to judge them other than their appearance. A few days later I would have the opportunity to see those SS men in action.

With all the propagandist fanfare of a generous conqueror, the SS organized a bread-distribution system. A large army truck loaded with bread would pull up at an intersection of a major thoroughfare and a loudspeaker would be set up. A speech to the following effect blared out at a volume that could be heard several blocks away: "The führer of the German Reich and the German people, due to the criminal neglect of the corrupt former regime of the now defunct Polish Republic, are compelled to provide food to the hungry population in this area." They explained also that anyone found speculating in food would be summarily executed.

When they decided that the accumulated mob was large enough, a motion-picture camera was set up and the distribution of bread began. The bread was so covered with fungus that it would not have been fit for consumption in normal times, but of course this did not show in the pictures the SS men took during its distribution. After deciding that they had filmed enough of the scene, they would rudely disperse the hungry mob using their rifle butts and go to repeat the process again in a different part of town.

I had occasion to observe this Nazi style of humane activity in several places in Praga. One such spectacle took place at the corner of Wilenska Street and Targowa, and another in front of the synagogue on Szeroka Street, across from the Red Cross building. In both places a handful of hungry Jews joined the line, but the Nazis were expecting them. With the help of some local hoodlums, the Jews were removed and beaten mercilessly.

While displaying to the world films revealing their generosity to the Polish people, the Nazis did not mention that with the occupation of the city, they also captured enormous quantities of grain, harvested just before the invasion, which still packed the warehouses. They immediately shipped all such goods to the Reich, leaving the local population with only the bare minimum and at the mercy of the elements during the first winter of that cruel war.

After several days of relative calm, we slowly began adapting ourselves to those drastically different conditions. Thus far there was little especially anti-Jewish activity by the Nazis, at least not visibly. But only a few days passed before a proclamation appeared that was directed at Jews only. The order was for Jews, under penalty of death, to deposit their radios at their respective police stations immediately. This was the first major specifically anti-Jewish act by the Nazis.

The order created quite a spectacle on the streets. Men and women, and even children, could be seen carrying radios of different size and vintage. Some of the large radios had to be transported by pushcarts and hand wagons. Generally the order was obeyed, but there were a few exceptions. I, for instance, decided to take a chance, for the time being at least, and held onto my shortwave radio.

The Polish right-wing extremists, the so-called O.N. group, immediately went into action on the Nazis' behalf by interpreting this anti-Jewish action as a pro-Polish attitude of the Germans. "You see," they said, "the Germans came here to help you to liberate yourselves from the Jewish pests, now and forever. They give you food, they don't take away your property, and they give you a free hand to do with the Jews as you please." Those Polish fascists may have gained some Nazi sympathy by their actions, but it was quite evident that the great majority of the Polish population remained aloof from those quislings. The Nazis, of course, took full advantage of the aid offered, particularly the assistance they were given in identifying Jews, initially for blackmail purposes only.

As conquerors, however, the Nazis were careful not to show any support for Mr. Dmowski, the leader of the Polish fascists. Dmowski was a sickly, rabid anti-Semite who before the war had been a constant menace to the Jewish population of Poland with his open calls for pogroms. His influence even extended to the universities, especially the University of Warsaw, where Jews had been strongly discriminated against before the war. The university had never been an institution of liberal and humane ideals, but in the late twenties and early thirties it had developed into a center of extreme chauvinism. In the last few years before the war, Jewish students were forced to take their seats on the left side of the aisle while the rest of the students sat on the right. This was how they solved the problem of providing separate but so-called equal education for the Jewish minority. But this was by no means all. Jewish students were pushed out of windows and subjected to severe beatings by mobs of students who periodically roamed the campus in search of victims. These sadistic students were the same ones who attacked individual Jews in the streets as an evening pastime.

Despite the close collaboration between the Nazis and the Polish fascists, there were some hidden misgivings between them, largely because of the built-in mistrust and subdued hatred between Poles and Germans that went back generations. In addition, there was a basic difference in their ideologies: whereas the Nazis' solution to the so-called Jewish question was total extermination, the Poles' brand of anti-Jewish ideology was such that their hatred for a Jew ceased on his acceptance of the Christian religion. Thus, the major difference was that Polish anti-Semitism had no racial overtones.

The next Nazi edict, this time applied to everyone, made listening to foreign radio broadcasts a crime punishable by death. The Germans installed large loudspeakers in several parts of the city as a substitute, supposedly to satisfy the people's requirement for daily news. The only news one heard, of course, was that which emanated from Joseph Goebbels's office.

It was no mystery to the Nazis that some of us disregarded their edict and continued to listen to foreign broadcasts, since that was the only way to get the truth. Catching the culprits was another matter, however, and the Nazis remained unable to solve that problem through the rest of the war.

The Nazis' first direct act of terror occurred in the suburb of Wawer, southeast of Praga, after someone supposedly had killed one or two German soldiers. In reprisal the Nazis assassinated a score of men, hanging some of their victims from street lanterns and leaving their bodies there for some time.

Next a system of rationing was instituted. For Jews food rations for items such as bread were set at one-fifth the rate established for others. Coupons for certain foods and several other products, such as garments and shoes, were not available to Jews at all.

Almost immediately the roundup of Jews for forced labor began. At first they randomly picked up Jews with strongly Semitic characteristics, such as men with beards and earlocks or with long and therefore characteristically Jewish clothing or people with black hair. But the education provided them by the local fascists soon allowed them to be much less selective. This was indeed a help, because they needed plenty of slave laborers to dismantle the partially damaged industrial plants. Most of the detainees were not accustomed to such labor, particularly those of the liberal professions, and some died on the job from exposure.

The Nazis stripped the factories clean of machinery and other equipment and promptly shipped off the bulk of the materials to Germany, acting as if the war were already over. Yet a German black market kept a considerable amount of that material from reaching its destination. Such diverted goods moved freely, since the Germans used military vehicles to transport their contraband.

Later, to harass and terrorize the Jews, the Nazis invented jobs that otherwise did not exist. In the process they discovered that a Jew, being in their eyes the lowest denominator, could be used for personal services such as cleaning their houses, their equipment, and, by no means least of all, their latrines.

Some semblance of normalcy slowly began to return to Warsaw, with a partial restoration of public utilities being one of the few hopeful signs. But it soon became apparent that several hundred thousand Jews could not share that hope.

The electric streetcars, the only mass transportation system in Warsaw, were already highly restricted the first day that they reappeared on the city streets. One car only was assigned for the Jewish population, and it was marked with a Star of David instead of a number. The fact that non-Jewish people were prohibited from using that car enabled the Nazis, without guessing, to grab Jews for forced labor whenever they wanted. The railway system was also being restored and was put back into operation on a limited basis. Jews were not allowed to use the trains at all. At first the German military were the only ones to ride by rail. But shortly thereafter the *Volksdeutsche,* or people of German extraction, were included as well.

Before the war the German population in Poland had been widely scattered across the country. Not unlike the rest of the Polish people, they were divided by their different occupations. Those living in cities and towns indulged in commerce and industry, whereas those in the countryside were active in farming. Most city Germans were integrated with the rest of the population to such an extent that the assimilation of their speech and behavior was almost complete, but the situation with the farmers was entirely different. They were living in completely separate villages and did not mix with the Polish farmers, who referred to them as "colonists." These colonists were by and large the best and most prosperous farmers. They had been living in Poland for a long time, with some claiming ancestry as far back as the time of King Kasimir the Great, who ruled in the fifteenth century. But they still had not acquired the Polish language, choosing instead to retain the ancient dialects of medieval Germany.

When the Nazis occupied Poland, everyone with even a trace of a German name was immediately registered and declared a *Volksdeutscher*. All German farmers from the Polish territory were then resettled into those western Polish lands that the Germans incorporated into Germany proper. The farms to which they were assigned had been confiscated from their former owners, the Polish farmers. Thus deprived of their property, the Polish farmers were shipped into the territory of the newly formed Generalgouvernement, or General Government of Poland, to work as slave laborers for the Germans. They were given no time to clear their property and were allowed to take only twenty pounds of their belongings with them. The *Volksdeutsche* were given all their property at no cost, down to the smallest household and business implements. In return those *Volksdeutsche* had only to give the Nazis young men for Hitler's police force and military.

Instead of being resettled, the city Germans (whose sons were particularly valuable as police officers, since they knew the land and its people) were repatterned in the German way. They were allowed to stay in cities and towns where they took over Jewish businesses.

# 2 KOSSOW

The trains again were running, but with one important difference: all railroad personnel were German—except for the fireman, who was a Pole. The arrogant Nazis thought that shoveling coal was beneath their dignity.

The forces initially assigned to enforce the ban on non-German use of the railways were largely inexperienced. Hence, anyone with some courage and knowledge of the German language was able to use the trains. But this was very risky. Non-German Gentiles, if caught, faced a beating and ejection from the train at the next stop. Jews, however, if detected as such, were beaten, tortured mercilessly, and then thrown off the moving train to a sure death. Under these circumstances, Jews elected to walk.

It was only about fifty miles to the little town of Kossow, where my mother, brother, and little son were living, so I decided to walk. Not bound to the highways, I used the side and country roads, managing to avoid being seen by military personnel until I had to pass through a town. A fifty-mile walk can be quite pleasant and interesting, particularly if it is one's first (and if there are no mountains to climb). It was strange indeed that of all the times I had traveled to Kossow by train, I did not recall noticing anything special about the area; perhaps it was the swiftness of the moving train that carried me through the gently rolling valley. All I had noticed were the tall, frequent church spires that dominated the lush countryside. But I soon found other sights worthy of interest. There were a couple of swift-running, crystal-clear streams that wound their way through the mosaic fields, only to be interrupted here and there by patterns of dark green pine groves. The streams emerged again on the other side, like silvery threads, rushing, resuming their eternal journey to the water's destiny, the faraway and beautiful green Baltic.

On their journey one of the streams crossed Mr. Schulthe's property. There it was blocked by an intricate system of dams and levees that provided power to Mr. Schulthe's flour mill. The mill was of only secondary interest to youngsters, whose main interest was the lake that the dams and levees formed. That lake provided the whole village with fishing and swimming facilities, and the Schulthe family never interfered with the activities of the youngsters who played on their property.

Late in the second day of my journey on foot, I approached the point where the railroad track began to curve in its semicircular approach to Kossow. From that point the road followed the railroad track for about half the remaining distance to town. The view from the road there was not as panoramic as from the train because of the high railroad embankment. The only sight to be seen was the tall spire of a bright red brick church, which told me I was only five miles from Kossow. The road began to slope down gently until it reached a little bridge over a creek. It then made a sharp left turn, crossed under the railroad tracks, and followed a straight course into town.

As I walked, I dreamily recalled the years of my youth when, as a little boy, I would spend the summers at my grandfather's place at one of the creeks. Life inside my grandfather's house was quite archaic, but I felt as free as a bird when outside playing with other children. I recalled roaming the fields, forests, and green meadows made lush by the rich black soil, fishing in the waters of the creek so clear that I could watch the fish grab the hook, or splashing carefree in the lake while swimming with the rest of the children.

I suddenly awoke to reality when I noticed a couple of Wehrmacht men walking down the road. I immediately assumed an air of self-assurance and continued to Kossow and my family, which I had not seen or heard from since the outbreak of the war. A few days before the invasion, I had telephoned my mother and asked her not to leave Kossow no matter what happened. I thought that a smaller town would most likely be less adversely affected than a city such as Warsaw.

I could detect no war damage as I approached Kossow. Even the railway station was intact. Nonetheless, my heart beat faster as I came closer to town and noticed that soldiers were staying in the farmers' homes. Apparently the Nazis had selected Kossow as a resting place for their troops.

Later I was to learn what had transpired in my family's town. The soldiers had put the peasants in the barns and made themselves comfortable in the houses. My family, too, was forced to leave their home and move into an old barn. Still, the initial aggression was not comparable to the brutal, un-dignified treatment to which the people had been subjected in Warsaw. Kossow owed this relative tranquility to the absence of SS (Defense Corps) troops and their trained killers, the SD (Security Service), as the German presence consisted largely of infantry and some artillery. However, the peace was disturbed occasionally when the SS and SD men from nearby Sokolow came to town on a robbing expedition. They usually robbed a few stores, filled up their trucks, beat up a few people, and left for the nearest town, where they sold the stolen merchandise. Then peace was restored until the next of their robbing missions, usually scheduled at one-month intervals. Eventually the local merchants started paying them off monthly, and they quit coming. But the relatively peaceful life for the Jewish people in Kossow changed abruptly with the arrival of the first civil authorities, the Gendarmerie. Although there were only four such constables assigned to Kossow, four Nazis were quite sufficient to keep such a small community in line at all times. Shortly after their arrival, the authorities summoned a group of prominent Jews and selected a few to represent the Jews of Kossow. There was very little business transacted between the two groups. Periodically these Germans demanded—and promptly received—monetary contributions. At other times they demanded laborers for the nearby town of Malkinia. However, with few exceptions, Kossow was still the best and safest place to live during those trying times. Eventually the troops slowly pulled out of town, thereby freeing some of the private homes for reoccupancy, my family's included. The remaining troops were rather friendly to the Jewish population, visiting and even dining with them on occasion. The reason for such an unusual relationship was the striking similarity between Yiddish, which was the Jewish language in Poland, and German. Living in Kossow, a remote place with no SS or SD troops to worry about and with a Gentile population that did not know German, those simple soldiers were attracted to places where they could be somewhat understood. I do not recall ever hearing them criticize Jews in any way, in the beginning.

# 3 My Decision

As yet I did not care to divulge my knowledge of the German language. I had no special reason not to at the time, other than a feeling of safety it provided me. I further decided not to reveal my identity as a Jew for the time being, and in this endeavor I secured the cooperation of the local Jewish community and its leaders. As it turned out later, the decision I made to hide my identity proved to be of great importance to me and many others. In doing so, I subconsciously laid the foundation for my future activity on behalf of my safety and, on many occasions, the safety of others.

There were no rules to go by. No handbook had ever been written or ever will be written that could be of use to a man who is hunted like a wild animal just because he was not born an Aryan. There were no rules of safety to follow to save one's life; all our choices had to be quick, ad hoc decisions made as each case presented itself. One important factor remained in my favor: I was born in Germany and spoke German without an accent. In Kossow, which was 80 percent Jewish and where practically everyone knew me, I had no valid reason to use this asset. Yes, I began to think of my fluent German as an asset, and then I thought of a way to make use of it. I decided to try posing as a *Volksdeutscher*.

Of course such deceit involved a great risk, but I believed the risk worthwhile if it would allow me to visit my friends in Warsaw and Praga. I also wanted to see what, if anything, had happened during my stay in Kossow. There were two men in Kossow who were separated from their families in Warsaw because of the war, and I had no problem convincing them to join me on a trip to the capital. One of the two men with me was another Jew, and we had agreed from the beginning that once on the train—even if in the same compartment—we would act as if we did not know each other.

Because the only rail connection between Kossow and Warsaw was through Malkinia, and because the bridge to Malkinia was out, we had to walk there to get a train to Warsaw. Malkinia was a railway hub located on the Bug River, which served as the so-called demarcation line between the Russians and Germans. I was familiar with that station from before the war because I used to change trains there on my way to Kossow.

It took only about three hours to reach Malkinia by foot. Once there, we learned that the train, which originated locally from this border station, would be leaving at 3:30 in the morning. It was sundown, and since it was toward the end of December, it was already very cold outside. This time of year was considered deep winter, and although it was not snowing yet, a strong northern wind made life quite miserable. Because the station was swarming with Germans, including SS troops, we decided to separate even before boarding the train. Fortunately we were not bothered by anyone.

The train pulled up to the passenger platform around 2:00 A.M. The Polish population was assigned to a few cattle cars with benches around the walls and two old fourth-class passenger cars. The rest of the train was reserved for Germans and *Volksdeutsche* only.

We took our seats in one of the passenger cars and were alone for the time being. After a while a German soldier walked into our compartment. We sat motionless with our hearts racing as he looked around slowly. His ice-cold stare pierced through us. Judging from his facial expression, he had obviously had more than just one drink that night. He pointed to the companion on my left and in a hoarse voice said, "Du, bist du Jude?" (Hey you, are you a Jew?) After my companion confirmed his identity in a voice quivering with fear, the soldier demanded that the man give him all the money that he had. Next he turned to me and asked the same question. I said no, and to strengthen my answer, I smiled slightly. He looked at me closely for a while, and then he started smiling also and asked me to join him in the war against the Jews and plutocrats. He got the same negative answer from the companion on my right and left the car seeming quite happy. The poor fellow on my left had given him all the money he had and now thanked God that it ended so peaceably.

That incident proved very important to me: it filled me with confidence in the future and gave me a certain feeling of security, albeit guarded security. I had discovered that my physiognomy was rather inconspicuous. From then on I reasoned that if I were able to adequately hide my fear, walk upright, and be prepared to lie about my identity with a straight face, then my life might not be as miserable as that of the average Jew. Though the risk I was willing to take was great, the alternative was much worse. My age was in my favor (I was then thirty-three), I was healthy and strong, and the challenge was fascinating.

It was snowing when we arrived at the Vilnius station in Praga that morning. I had asked the janitor to take care of my apartment on Brukowa Street while I was away, and I found it in good condition on my return. But in my absence many important events had taken place, especially among the Jewish population. The Nazis had rapidly herded into Warsaw all the Jews from the countless surrounding communities, thereby choking the already overcrowded city. In barely three months their population had increased to one-half million. The great influx of people also included those from the former western Polish territory that had been unceremoniously incorporated into the Reich.

After a short period of time, the Nazis organized a Jewish governing body that they called the "Judenrat." This allowed the Nazis to control Jews with the help of other Jews. Along with performing certain limited functions, the so-called counselors of the Judenrat were obliged to furnish the Nazis with a daily supply of slave labor (despite the fact that Nazis were still breaking into Jewish homes and dragging away their victims). It was obvious that the Judenrat was created only to serve as a handmaiden in the oppression and exploitation of the Jews. The counselors may have thought otherwise, however.

A Judenrat police force was organized, the officers clad in dark uniforms with arm bands displaying the Star of David. The Nazis required that the arm band be yellow, the same color used in the ancient ghettos. These policemen carried sticks rather than firearms. The police force was supposed to be open to all volunteers, but because the Judenrat police were immune from forced labor, it turned out to be a privileged group consisting of those who had connections or money. At first most men who bought themselves into the force were from well-to-do families and belonged to the liberal professions. Their professional knowledge was of no use to them, however, since Hitler deprived the Jews of any opportunity to engage in public practice. Those young intellectuals were quite aware of what to expect from the Nazis should they end up in a slave labor camp, especially those who earlier had been caught on the street during a *Razzia* (a police raid in which everyone in sight was grabbed indiscriminately for slave labor). At first they gratefully accepted the opportunity to avoid such labor and acted with restraint. But under nearly any conceivable condition there is a built-in element of corruption, and before long corruption made itself felt here, too, at first in a small way. Providing food and shelter for the displaced people was an undertaking of major proportion for the Judenrat, who used the police force to maintain order. Those fine boys, products of the upper crust of Jewish society, suddenly discovered that they were in a position not just to save themselves from labor. Now they could also cash in on the misery of the less fortunate without fear of punishment. Later they would sell freedom from labor camps, and later still they would accept bribes to exclude people from being transported eastward for extermination.

The Nazis' next move was to force Jews to register under penalty of death. All Jews between the ages of twelve and seventy were compelled to register. That registration was followed by a proclamation ordering the Jews to wear white arm bands with a blue Star of David. I did not comply with either of those orders. I was quite aware of the consequences, but I could not submit to such barbaric treatment and was determined to go underground if necessary.

Soon the anti-Jewish proclamations began to appear weekly and then so often that I quit reading them. It was about that time that I found it opportune to dispose of my shortwave radio. Thanks to a good neighbor, however, I was not deprived of the opportunity to listen to uncensored news. This neighbor opened his house to men like myself so that we would not lose contact with the outside world. He was a fine gentleman whose name—Wilhelm Spicmacher—could not have been more German had he been born in Berlin.

Wilhelm Spicmacher, an older, semiretired gentleman, was of German extraction but could not speak a word of German. His wife, Martha, was of Polish stock. He had two sons who were both my good friends and trustworthy patriots, as well as two daughters. With a name like his, Spicmacher did not have to go to the authorities to register as a *Volksdeutscher;* the Nazis looked him up immediately and invited him to join with the other *Volksdeutsche* in the German community. Because he did what they asked of him, we were able to use his home as a BBC reception station. This was how we managed to get our daily news from London. Of course, we took all necessary precautions to ensure that he and his family would not be endangered.

Spicmacher helped me in another way as well. It was now late in the spring of 1940, and I had not seen my family since December 1939. I wanted to travel by rail this time, since the highways were no longer safe, but I needed some moral support. I approached Spicmacher with a proposition to join me on a trip to Kossow. Knowing that I would feel safer in the company of a *Volksdeutscher,* even one who spoke no German, he gladly consented to help.

We departed the following Saturday. As it turned out, there was not one vacant seat in the cars earmarked for Poles, and the rest of the train, which was reserved for the Germans, was practically empty. Spicmacher was definitely not the assertive type, so the burden of making a quick decision fell on me. His presence, however, gave me enough courage to walk into one of those German cars and ask the conductor whether I might take a seat in that car. The conductor, who stood blocking the doorway, answered by asking me whether I was a German. I answered jokingly that I was something very close to it. He laughed and stepped aside to let us in. It all seemed so easy that I almost forgot the danger of the situation. As I began to realize what was at stake, I became really frightened. I noticed that Spicmacher was no less fearful.

About halfway to our destination the same conductor came into our compartment to check our tickets. It was merely a routine check, but under our traveling conditions nothing was routine. He pointed at Spicmacher and asked whether he too was a German (evidently he had no doubt about me). I said to the conductor, "Natürlich mein Freund Herr Spicmacher ist Deutscher" (Naturally my friend Mr. Spicmacher is a German), and turning to my friend, I said, "Willie bitte zeige dem Konductor deine Kennkarte." I was sure that Mr. Spicmacher understood the last word of my sentence. While he was reaching into his pocket for his identity card, the conductor motioned for him to leave it alone. Everything seemed fine to him, and he said good-bye as he left the car. That episode again demonstrated to me unquestionably that, in certain circumstances, audacity is a prerequisite to success.

After that trip I began to travel to Kossow alone quite often, eventually on a weekly basis. So far my philosophy of nonsubmission had paid off. Nonetheless, every time I crossed that road, I crossed my fingers. Only I knew how frightened I was, and I was careful not to divulge that secret.

About the time I resumed my trips to Kossow, rumors began to circulate that the Jewish population of Warsaw would be separated from the rest of the people. We heard too that the Germans were already building masonry walls in different parts of the city. The first reports were treated as simple gossip, which we had in abundance. I therefore decided to make a trip across the city to see what, if anything, was going on. I did see some walls going up here and there but could not understand the reason for them. I asked a mason at one site what the walls were for, but he either did not know or did not want to tell me.

Just about the same time, the news that Hitler had invaded Norway and Denmark awoke some hope that this could be the beginning of the end of the hated Nazis. But once more, disappointment followed. Hitler had done it again . . . and gotten away with it.

Shortly afterward came the biggest news of all: France had been invaded. We thought that would never happen. Surely France, with Great Britain on its side, would never fall to the Nazis. But after a few weeks, we knew that France too was doomed.

The shock of the quick Nazi victory over France is hard to describe. Our thoughts turned back to September 1939, when Poland had been invaded. Historically there had been a long, close, and friendly relationship between France and Poland, although that friendship had been marred somewhat during the period of flirtation between the Smigly-Rydz regime and Germany. It was hard to find an educated Pole who did not speak French, which was considered almost a second national tongue. Sentimentality set aside, one cold fact remained: the hope of regaining independence any time soon had been eliminated.

The increased feeling of insecurity, combined with the necessity of procuring the minimum amount of food required to sustain life, caused many people to dispose of whatever valuables they had managed to hide from the Nazis. This led to the development of a brisk black market. Businessmen and artisans also had been able to hide some of their merchandise and materials, from which they produced finished products in the relative safety of their cellars. Two of my close friends fit in this category: one owned a furrier business, and the other a jewelry business, before the outbreak of the war.

There were plenty of jobs around (except for Jews), but most were related to the Nazi war effort, and I was not ready to help the enemy unless forced to do so. Instead I joined with my two friends in the smuggling business. Each time I traveled into the countryside, I sold their goods to the farmers and purchased food to bring back to my friends in Warsaw. My willingness and ability to take risks were thus put to a profitable use.

Traveling almost every week gave me the opportunity to see things of which most people, particularly Jews, were not aware. I was especially intrigued by the defense preparations going on in the vicinity of Warsaw during the summer of 1940. Some places were camouflaged, while others were painted with a special color, such as the dark blue that covered the railroad station windows. No one (except of course the Nazis) knew what enemy the concrete bunkers were supposed to deter.

In midsummer of 1940 those mysterious walls in Warsaw began to go up at a faster pace. What in the spring had appeared to be a crossword puzzle with scattered pieces now began to look like a medieval fortress. But no medieval fortress had ever covered so much territory. In some places the walls ran down the centers of streets right between the streetcar tracks. In other places whole rows of apartment buildings had their gates blocked up with bricks.

One day, in the early fall of 1940, an edict appeared signed by Hans Frank, who was the Nazi governor general of the Generalgouvernement. It stated: "Effective immediately, the Jews who are now scattered throughout the city and the surrounding area are ordered, under penalty of death, to make arrangements to move to the sector especially provided for them. Those Jews found after the fifteenth of October outside the Jewish sector will be shot on sight." Even for the efficient Nazis, however, the time allotted for the resettlement of such a large number of people turned out to be too short. It was thus necessary to postpone the deadline until November 15.

A few days after that proclamation, an angry article appeared in a German newspaper printed in Warsaw, the *Warschauer Zeitung*, complaining that the Jews and plutocrats were spreading rumors—intended to besmirch the name of the Germans—that the Jews were being pressed into a so-called ghetto. Nothing, claimed the German paper, could be further from the truth. That sector arrangement had nothing to do with a ghetto; it was intended as a place where Jews could live in peace and security and further their cultural heritage, a place where the Germans could protect the Jews from their Polish neighbors. After that famous article appeared, rumors circulated that anyone mentioning the term *ghetto* would be summarily executed.

The resettlement took place on an exchange basis. Any Gentile living in the now official Jewish sector had to move out to make room for incoming Jews. I too decided to exchange my apartment with a family from inside the ghetto, although I did not intend to live there. Living in a ghetto was tantamount to living in a jail or worse, particularly under the Nazis. It made me furious just to think about it.

The first and only night I spent in the ghetto, November 15, 1940, was the night after I had moved my furniture. My new residence was located close to a major checkpoint at the corner of Pawia and Okopowa Streets. The next morning I walked outside and noticed a large crowd assembled near a group of German police who were blocking the exit. The haste with which the Nazis acted in sealing the ghetto had caught many Gentiles inside, and these people were now concentrated at the exit waiting for passage out. I too approached that point and waited with a made-up excuse. In the meantime I discovered that the reason for the delay was that the German police did not know what to do. They kept everyone there until they received the order to let only the Gentiles through. I told them that I was a Gentile and that I had not quite been able to leave the day before. I was let out without problem, and for the time being I stayed with my friends in Praga.

The ghetto was now an indisputable fact. From that time on, the ghetto was closed, but the Nazis were unable to seal it hermetically for a technical reason: to reach a major railroad station, they had to run the streetcars through the ghetto. To solve that problem, the Nazis ordered the streetcar operators to drive through the ghetto at a high rate of speed without stopping. It was impossible to obey that order, however, because the Nazi bigwigs—who lived mostly in the newer sections of the capital, with its wide promenades—failed to take into consideration the narrow width of the ghetto streets and the tight curves at their intersections, where slowing down to almost a complete stop was imperative. I used that streetcar to enter and leave the ghetto at least once a week, smuggling out merchandise and returning with food for several friends who by now needed help badly. One in particular was the wife of a good friend who never returned home from the war. They had a little girl my son's age.

The Polish police, of course, knew about the streetcar traffic problems within the ghetto. After the collapse of Poland, they had come out of hiding and had reported to the Nazis for service. In their wildest dreams the Nazis could not have hoped for more loyal elements than the Polish police. They turned out to be far better at collaboration than were the police in any other conquered territory. At first the Nazis ordered a Polish police officer to be placed on each of the streetcars, but they soon discovered that one man was not enough to keep things under control. Next they tried placing an officer on each of the four platforms. But this still did not succeed in stopping the traffic to and from the ghetto.

Faced with such a colossal problem, they decided to eliminate the streetcar traffic from the ghetto altogether. To accomplish this they reduced the size of the ghetto by taking out one street and then used that street for streetcar traffic after blocking up the cross streets with masonry. Thus, the streetcar problem was finally solved, and the one-half million or more Jews inside the ghetto were faced with a ten-foot-high brick wall capped with broken glass. To maintain contact with the rest of the city, the inhabitants made holes in the wall here and there. The Polish police were aware of this, however, and had to be bribed so that these holes could be used to supply the people inside. Such holes were mainly reserved for professional smugglers only. I had to pay dearly for help to get in, but I got in—not once a week anymore, but every two weeks—no matter what the price.

Mijały dni w trwożnym oczekiwaniu
tej katastrofy, która się systematy-
cznie również i do nas zbliżała.
Codziennie inna miejscowość objętą
została tą „akcją" mordercą.
Nie przerywając tej szlachetnej robo-
ty w Warszawie. Ironia losu, albo
zwierzęca perfidja, jak kto woli,
gdyż podczas tej akcji wymordowują
ej żydów, urządzili w Generalnym
Gubernatorstwie tak zwaną:
„Kulturwoche"! rozdmuchaną z
wprzęgnięciem ogromnej maszyny
propagandowej, a w tym trzeba
im przyznać, byli mistrzami.
20-go sierpnia 1942 roku odbyła się
narada w Siedlcach, część wy-
wieźli do Treblinki, resztę zaś

Sample page from Hermann Wygoda's original memoirs, which he wrote in Polish in 1945. The author translated the document into English twenty years later.

Hermann Wygoda, around 1908, holding the hand of his mother, Chana. One of Chana's sisters stands to Hermann's left.

Leon Wygoda, Hermann's younger brother, with their mother in an undated photograph.

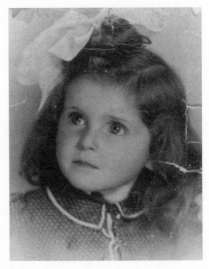

Two photographs that the author carried with him throughout the war. The boy is his son, Samuel, and the girl is the daughter of a friend killed during the Nazi invasion of Poland.

Kossow, Poland, in an undated photograph. The author's family lived in this small town, located seven miles from Treblinka. Photo courtesy of Rivka Barlev.

Stanislaw Gorczyca, Polish postal worker, who hid the author at his home in Warsaw in 1942. Photo courtesy of Paul Peregal.

Wilhelm and Martha Spicmacher in an undated photograph.

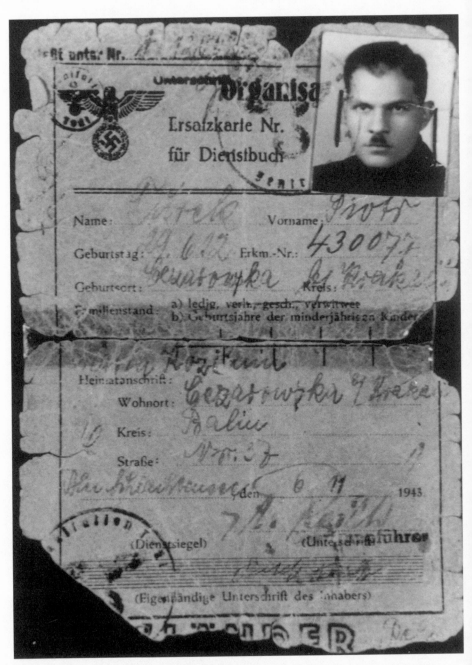

Leon Peregal, the author's companion from 1942 to 1944, pictured on his fraudulent OT ("Organisation Todt") identity card from 1943. Photo courtesy of Paul Peregal.

# 4 My Brother Is Taken, Again

All through the fall and winter of 1940, the Nazis were busy constructing revetments, bunkers, and tank traps not far from the railroad tracks, particularly in the area between the Bug River demarcation line and Warsaw. By spring 1941 the Nazis already were talking openly about an inevitable war with the Soviet Union, and in Kossow the Germans were ready for such a war by the beginning of May.

Kossow, only about seven miles from the border, became a Nazi divisional headquarters used to prepare for the invasion. Several batteries of heavy artillery were in place, and infantry detachments were camped in surrounding farms, small patches of forest, and nearby villages. All this was visible from town.

On the evening of June 21, we knew that the attack would begin the following morning, the longest day of the year in that part of the world. As I prepared to retire for the night, my thoughts were of the far-reaching consequences, possibly for all humanity, of this upcoming major event. It took me quite a while to fall asleep, and it must have been far into the night when I finally yielded to my heavily laden eyelids and plunged into a world of dreams.

The sound of airplanes woke me, and I went outside to look up into the sky. All the windows in the houses around me were trembling, as was the ground beneath my feet. In the dim twilight I could distinguish a great air armada moving in a northeasterly direction. It was impossible to count so many planes.

At the same time the heavy artillery let loose with all they had, almost drowning out the sound of the planes. It continued that way for several hours until the noise gradually began moving farther away. It was evident from the diminishing sound of the exploding artillery shells that the Germans were making quick progress. By nightfall all the sounds had died down, and most of the Nazis were gone from Kossow.

The next morning a single Soviet plane, which was subsequently shot down, flew over Kossow and dropped some bombs that killed a few people. That was the extent of the war in Kossow. The following day we saw a large column of Russians who were supposedly prisoners of war. What we actually had seen was a large group of people ranging in age from ten to over seventy with what appeared to be Russian border patrol soldiers sprinkled in here and there.

Gestapo men began to show up in Kossow a few days after the Russians had been pushed away from the border. They arrested a prominent non-Jewish man, and his family was not told where he was taken or with what he had been charged. Several weeks later his wife received a notice from the Gestapo that her late husband was the victim of an accident and that for the sum of 100 marks his remains would be shipped to her in an urn. To us, this meant only one thing—the little town of Kossow already had its own spy.

That shock was sufficient to paralyze the community for a long time. Everyone became a suspect. Everyone was overcome with fear and no longer knew in whom to confide. We had to observe the utmost caution during our incipient underground meetings. Still, after several weeks of high tension and great fear, community life became again as normal as life could under the Nazis.

One day in the late fall of 1941, a large truck and a passenger car drove up in the middle of town and parked in front of the Judenrat office. I was in the barbershop across the street, watching through the drapes. From the car stepped four SS officers in long green leather coats, each with a long whip dangling from his side. They looked around for a while and then proceeded into the Judenrat office. The truck was fully loaded with SD men in black uniforms.

Soon the SD men scattered throughout the town. As I found out later, they had lists of all the Jewish craftsmen in Kossow. They were particularly interested in carpenters, plumbers, painters, and electricians. The men were rounded up and assembled in front of the Judenrat office, where Mr. Liberman, the head of the Kossow Judenrat, told them that they were being taken to a nearby construction project to work. He also told them that they should consider themselves as volunteer workers, they would be paid, and they would be free three days of every month to come home to their families. Standing there among the others was my brother, Leon, a cabinetmaker by trade.

The previous year I had gotten him out of a camp for Polish prisoners of war, a camp set up in Lublin especially for Jews. When I had received the first word of his whereabouts in the spring of 1940, I promptly went to Lublin and contacted him at the camp. The few minutes we had together were sufficient to work out a plan for getting him out. Every morning the Nazi guards marched the prisoners across the city through the narrow, winding streets of the Jewish sector to work at some warehouses. We agreed that the following morning, as the men were being assembled for the march, Leon would try to stay in the last row of the column. At my signal, he was to quickly jump out of the column and I would take care of the rest.

I then went back to town and bought an old suit of clothes, a shirt, and a pair of shoes, which I deposited at a store along the prisoners' route. I bought two railroad tickets to Warsaw for the next day, and then I rested.

The next morning I went back to the vicinity of the camp but remained at a safe distance so that the guards would not see me. It was a nerve-racking undertaking, but so was everyday life under the Nazi regime. This undertaking promised to be rewarding, however, and to an extent even fascinating.

Soon I saw the prisoners assembling on the camp grounds. They were divided into two columns, each of approximately regular company strength. The Nazis were so sure of themselves that they never had more than one soldier with each column. As they marched out the gate, I followed at a close enough distance so that my brother could see me. As we had agreed, he was in the last row of the second column. He noticed me as we came closer to town.

I pulled ahead of the column and stopped on the corner in front of the store where I had hidden the clothing. I took my place beside several Jewish men who had previously agreed to help us and who had been waiting at the edge of the sidewalk and the cobblestone street. Our group practically covered the whole width of the sidewalk. I watched as the column approached and gave Leon the signal as soon as he was next to me. He quickly jumped over and entered the store. Before following him inside, I waited until the column was out of sight. We met at the rear of the store and left for the railway station as quickly as possible, with Leon wearing the clothes I had bought the day before. Leon's regular features and almost flaxen hair caused no concern among the Nazis, and thus we were able to make the journey with no complications whatsoever.

Now, as I looked at him standing in front of the Judenrat office surrounded by black-clothed SD men, I wondered whether he would have a second chance. To our surprise, however, the boys returned home after an absence of only several weeks. The Nazis had put them to work assembling barracks and office buildings in a newly organized camp in nearby Treblinka. They had been told that it was going to be a rehabilitation camp for alcoholics and common criminals.

Beginning at that period the Nazis were steady visitors to Kossow, and even the black-clothed ones would on occasion visit the town, apparently for no special reason.

I returned to my routine business, traveling to Warsaw once every two weeks to bring out merchandise and sell it. Traveling, of course, was the only routine part. Entry and exit from the ghetto was becoming a major problem, not only in getting in and out safely, but also in having the strength to want to go there again.

People in the ghetto began to die rapidly and in progressively greater numbers. The utilities inside the ghetto were cut off altogether during the winter of 1941–42, and food rations were practically nonexistent. People simply lay down on the sidewalks and died a terrible death from starvation.

The progress of death could be observed on its poor victims daily. As a rule they did not come out into the street until they were completely destitute, and even then some would not stretch out their hands to beg. At first you saw them standing but holding onto a wall from weakness. They stood in silence, hoping perhaps that a charitable individual would notice their plight and offer help in some way. Such expectation was in vain; there was no chance for such miracles. Death was slow in coming. Before long holding onto the wall required too much effort for their weakened bodies, and they had to sit down. Soon even this was impossible, and they had to lie down, never again to stand up on their feet. By then all that was left was skin covering bones. The final stage of their mute martyrdom began as they lost consciousness and swelled up like balloons. After that some kind person, who would likely be a candidate for the same fate the following week or sooner, covered them up with paper. The next day their bodies were picked up by men with pushcarts.

I saw the Hitler Jugend, visiting the ghetto under the guidance of their SS leaders, taking pictures of those skeletons stretched out on the sidewalks, and I wondered whether, after returning home, those children sat with their parents at the dinner table discussing the things they had seen in Warsaw.

Although it was heartbreaking and frustrating to look at such terrible things, it was more exasperating to witness little children sitting half-naked, their shrunken faces blue-black in the winter's cold. They looked like miniature skeletons, frozen, immobile, the only moving parts being the glassy eyes, set deep in bony sockets with an expression of hopeful expectation.

As I walked through the streets of the Warsaw ghetto that winter, I wondered whether God knew what was going on beneath Him on this troubled earth. The only analogy I could find in history was perhaps the pogrom of the Jews in Alexandria at the time of the Roman governor Flaccus, as reported by Philo Judaeus, or the massacre of the Armenians by the Turks during World War I.

In all fairness, it must be said that in the beginning those who were starving got some help from passersby, but it was not enough to keep them alive. With the passage of time, however, the population became accustomed to that sight and usually passed by those half-corpses without even looking. There was a large restaurant in the center of the ghetto on the corner of Karmelicka and Nowolipie Streets. It was considered one of the better ones, and it was always busy and full of the so-called well-to-do individuals of the ghetto. Some of the poor hung around outside the restaurant hoping to get a little help from the patrons. Seldom did that work. I watched people come out of that restaurant expressing satisfaction at being well fed and not even glance at those poor men, women, and children who had been waiting sometimes for hours to get help.

Every trip I made into the ghetto became a tragedy for me. I usually came out with such a broken heart that I was pushed nearly to the point of having a nervous breakdown. Nonetheless, the ghetto continued to pull me in like a magnet. My friends needed my help, and I believed that was reason enough to keep going there.

# 5 Twice Arrested

I returned to Kossow in February 1942. One evening, quite unexpectedly, while I was visiting some friends, the local Polish police came into their home and arrested me.

At the police station I was questioned: "What do you do for a living? What is your income?" and so on. I knew that local gossip had me getting rich because I was selling gold, diamonds, and furs. It did not dawn on those policemen that I might be working for someone else on a commission basis, which I was. They also indicated that it was a crime not to wear the Jewish arm band with the Star of David. My suggestion that I expected such statements from a Nazi policeman but not from a Pole brought me a beating and landed me in jail. I guessed that they wanted money, but I was not yet prepared to pay if I did not have to.

The following day I was taken by train to Sokolow, a much larger town located fifteen miles to the south. Instead of taking me directly to the Sokolow jail, the policeman in charge took a roundabout way from the railroad station to town so that he could stop at his residence first. There I was given to understand that, for a price, he had the authority to let me go. Somehow I did not trust him, so I let the offer pass. After a few hours, he took me back to the station, and we boarded a train to return to Kossow. A few days later they took me back to Sokolow. This time they put me in the Sokolow ghetto, where I was told to remain until further notice.

That incident affected my immediate plans and behavior significantly.

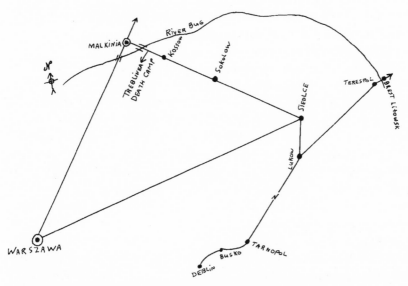

Author's map showing the rail lines linking the Polish cities and towns he traveled between 1939 and 1943.

Filled with deep-seated fear, I was unable to leave the ghetto for a while. I felt like a bird whose wings had suddenly been clipped. Those weeks in the Sokolow ghetto were not completely wasted, however, for it was then that I first met Leon Peregal, a former prisoner of war who had been recently released from a POW camp in Germany. Although I did not know it at the time, Leon was to play a major role in my life to follow.

After a few weeks I regained enough courage to make another trip to Warsaw. Rather than chance an encounter at the local railway station, I rode a bicycle to the next station along the line to Warsaw. That routed my trip through Siedlce, which was a major railway hub much busier than Malkinia to the north. This new route made the trip somewhat longer but much safer for me. Traveling made me feel free again.

As a rule my first stop would be the Spicmachers' apartment in Praga, where I would learn the latest local and international news. The news at the time was encouraging, since the situation at the front had changed considerably. Only a short time before, Hitler had promised the German people that he would bring their boys home for Christmas, thus implying that the war with the Russians would be over by then. But it was now early spring of 1942, and the Nazis seemed farther away from Moscow than they had been in December. Nonetheless, although the news from the front began to be a spirit

lifter, it was generally conceded that such developments were of little consequence for the Jewish population, since the Nazi extermination machine was
just getting into full swing.

I had two places in Warsaw where I could spend unlimited time at my
own discretion. One, a small house belonging to my good friend Stanislaw
Gorczyca, was located south of Praga in the suburb of Wawer. The other was
an apartment on the opposite side of the city in the suburb of Wola; I acquired this Mlynarska Street hideout also through the efforts of Stanislaw.

The latest news in Warsaw was the most recent edict by the Nazis, directed
to the Gentile population living outside the ghetto. It declared that any Gentile found hiding, or possessing knowledge of anyone hiding, a member of
the Jewish race would be summarily executed, together with his entire family. With that, I quit going to my former residence in Praga because too many
people knew me there. Some, I felt, did not know me well enough to be trustworthy under such conditions. Stanislaw told me to disregard the edict and
move in with him and his family if I desired. It was a wonderful feeling to
know that I had such a good friend.

I now could find no logical explanation for my continued desire to visit
the Warsaw ghetto, because the little girl to whom I regularly brought food
had died since my last visit, and I had no other close friends or blood rela-
tives there. The only people I knew fairly well were the family of Dr. Mandel,
a dentist who lived in an apartment across the hall from the place into which
I had moved my belongings during the exchange. Both he and his wife were
highly sophisticated, well read, and great lovers of music. Ironically, just before the start of the war, they had returned to Poland from Venezuela because
they missed the cultural atmosphere of Warsaw. Now their only daughter and
her husband were in a slave labor camp.

The Nazis seldom told the truth, but from the evidence thus far I knew
that this was the beginning of the extermination of the Jews in Europe. Still,
the Nazis managed to cover up their crimes by misinforming the people. Dr.
Mandel thought that the Nazis were attempting to eliminate only the para-
sitical elements among the Jews by a selective system of extermination. The
explanation Dr. Mandel gave was exactly what I had read some time ago in
the Nazi mouthpiece the *Warschauer Zeitung*. By dropping hints in their news
media implying that intellectuals would be excluded from extermination, the
Nazis hoped to placate the intelligentsia and secure their cooperation in the
"final solution" of the Jewish question. Dr. Mandel was so sure of himself
that he refused to go into the woods with me, as I asked him to do. He felt
more secure in the ghetto than outside it. Besides, who was I to argue with a
well-educated and otherwise intelligent man?

It was time again for me to return to Sokolow; shortly after my arrival there, I was called to appear at the office of the Judenrat. I failed to appear as summoned, and the next morning I was unceremoniously arrested by a smartly dressed Jewish policeman named Lipschitz and thrown into an improvised jail located in the town's only synagogue. Among many other things, praying was forbidden for Jews, and the Nazis had converted the synagogues into Jewish government buildings for the Judenrat. Since no government can exist without a jail, they had converted what seemed to have been a Talmud Torah, or religious school, into a prison.

There I was behind the wooden bars, neither told nor asked anything for quite a while. Finally, speaking through a window, I managed to ask a passerby to notify my friends where I was. With their help, I learned that my destination was a slave labor camp in the swamps of Pinsk. The leaders of the Judenrat claimed that they had arrested me because they had to meet the quota requested by Dr. Hermann, the *Kreisleiter* (district governor) of the Sokolow region. Some time later they hinted to my friends that—for a certain price—they could spare me the inconvenience by finding a substitute.

There was no alternative left to consider; once a man was thrown into that camp in the swamps, he never left it alive. After I agreed to submit to their extortion, the rest was automatic: an appearance before Mr. Finkelstein, the president of the Sokolow Judenrat.

Without looking up from his desk, Mr. Finkelstein began to complain about the hard times we were living through under the Nazis. After that preliminary statement, he got to the point and asked me how much I was willing to pay for the privilege of being left in peace. Although I was flabbergasted by such unmitigated blackmail, I answered that I thought the question to be not how much I was willing to give but rather how much I was able to pay. He retorted impatiently, "Well, how much are you able to pay?" We did some horse-trading and arrived at the nominal sum of 5,000 zloty ($600) in Polish currency, an amount I thought reasonable, considering the alternative. That incident again jolted my confidence, and I lost interest in any activity for some time.

The sudden, partially self-imposed inactivity almost completely enveloped me in a feeling of aggravated despair. First of all, in Sokolow I was dependent solely on gossip. The only news available was what the German newspapers printed, and it was depressing to read of nothing but German victories. Worse yet, I was continuously concerned for my safety in that overstuffed and fenced-in ghetto. The fear of being confronted in the dark of the night by a sudden attack from the SS and their helpers, the SD killers, of being turned into a helpless victim with almost no way of escape, caused me sleepless nights and a nearly total nervous breakdown. From the beginning of the German occupation, my nervous system had been strained by my dangerous way of life. My two recent arrests only added to a terrible mental state.

Strange thoughts entered my mind during those nights and even sometimes during the day. I was thinking of the unfortunate people already condemned to die on the gallows but forced to wait for the final decision while confined to a dark cell. But just as quickly I rejected such dreary thoughts: "*No*, and a thousand times *no!*" I said out loud to myself. "Am I not a fighter? *No*, I shall not submit!" I decided to continue to fight regardless of what happened. I had to get out of that ghetto as quickly as possible, and I left for Warsaw immediately. It was toward the end of July 1942.

On my arrival, my friend Stan informed me that something unusual was taking place in Warsaw and warned me to be extremely cautious if I wanted to enter the ghetto. He had heard that the Nazis were building some kind of partitions in the general area of the Danziger railroad station, which was the station closest to the ghetto. Furthermore, he said that all available railroad freight cars were being assembled there, and strangely, the Nazis were busy closing all the air vents in those cars with barbed wire and heavy boards nailed from the outside.

Such actions were rather mysterious, so I decided to check my underground ghetto entry. Finding it still operational, I went inside once again. This time the situation was different. There was much more tension in the air, and there were more German patrols circling the area. Whenever a patrol car came into sight, everyone, including myself, ran for cover. Lately those patrols had been shooting into the crowd indiscriminately.

After entering the ghetto, I usually had to cross Nalewki Street before going to Nowolipki Street. While crossing, on my left, down the road by a park named Ogrod Krasinskich, I noticed a large mass of people being led by what at a distance looked like Nazi police. All over the area people were running like mad. I ran too, across the street and through a doorway. I barely made it. Those inside were already locking the doors, although the courtyard and doorway were full of people. I could hear everyone's heartbeats.

There were peepholes in the doors of that building, but to look through a hole required both luck and agility in such a crowd of people. Somehow I managed to get a glimpse for a few seconds. The column I saw marching in the direction of the Danziger railroad station was composed of Jewish men and women, approximately eighteen or twenty abreast and very close together. They were flanked by Nazi guards with rifles at the ready and fixed with bayonets. The march lasted for about forty minutes or so, and when the last column was out of sight, someone opened the door and we all went out into the street. I doubted the wisdom of my decision to be there and hesitated—but then turned west on Nowolipke Street anyway.

Suddenly the crowd started running again, and I followed as before. This time I wound up in a doorway on the corner of Nalewki Street in a much smaller crowd, so I could watch the street through the peephole to my heart's desire. I noticed a passenger car drive by and stop only a few feet from our building. The car carried three SS men and a civilian. The civilian and two of the SS got out, but I could see nothing more from my vantage point. After a while I heard a shot and saw the two SS men get back into the car and drive off in the direction from which they had come.

When the Nazis were out of sight, we went into the street to see what had happened next door. We found a man lying dead, face down, with blood running from behind his ear (according to Nazi propaganda, killing with a shot in the back of the head was supposed to be an exclusive monopoly of the Russian Bolsheviks). He was still quivering. Someone turned him over to see his face, and I could see that he was quite young. I was told by the people from that area that such things had been going on almost every day but that usually the Nazis killed their victims outside the ghetto and then threw their corpses back in over the wall.

This last tragic incident made me change my mind. I turned around and left as quickly as I could, never to return to the ghetto.

However, my trip back to Praga was not completely free of problems. Usually I was very alert and made sure I was not followed, but this time I failed to see that someone was tailing me at a distance. I don't know where he started following me, but he was right behind me when I entered the streetcar on my way to Praga. As I took my place on the platform in the rear of the car, this young fellow in his late teens made it a point not to become separated from me. He looked at me continuously, all the time mumbling something under his breath long enough and loud enough for me to hear and for him to let me know that I was the object of his attention. His behavior told me that he was not quite sure about me and that he most likely was fishing in the dark. He'd probably seen me coming out of the ghetto and decided to take a chance. There were plenty of parasites like him who made a habit of cashing in on the misery of others. Their system was simple. They believed that if their judgment was right, that if their victim was Jewish, then sooner or later he would succumb to their inexorable pressure. Once they got their prey to panic, then their efforts of blackmail and terror usually paid off handsomely. They robbed him of everything he had and let him go free, only to direct the Nazis to him. Apparently they reasoned that if they called the Nazis first, they would be deprived of their loot, since the Nazis, too, were experts in robbing.

Throughout the trip I maintained my icy posture. My behavior indicated that either I did not hear his mumbling or I did not want to hear it. At a stop where a German soldier entered the car, I felt that young fellow's intense study of my face, searching for some change in my expression. But at the soldier's entry, he stopped his mumbling, and I played it calm too.

When the car passed St. John's Catholic Church, located on the Krakowskie Przedmiescie, I dutifully raised my hat like any good Catholic, in keeping with the age-old tradition. I knew that some people even crossed themselves on such occasions, but I followed the majority rule, knowing that I could not afford to make any mistakes or to show any hesitation or expression of less than total self-confidence. The young man was still near me when we crossed the Kierbedzia Bridge, but crossing the river got him away from his usual area of operation and into one with which I was quite familiar. I also had friends there. His perseverance indicated that he thought he really had something and expected to make quite a killing.

In the second block past the bridge there was a hospital and a large double-spire church on the right side of the street, with an east-west street running between them. The hospital, as well as the church, had been partly bombed out in 1939, and most of the buildings in the area were either partially or completely in ruins. I began to breath easier since I was in my territory. I got out of the streetcar at the church stop, although I still had no plan. I wanted to see whether he would follow me, and follow me he did. I walked east toward Szeroka Street, which ran from the river to Targowa Street, the main thoroughfare of Praga.

Since this part of the suburb was practically deserted, I could have either killed him outright or simply beat him up without fear of intervention. Undoubtedly his concentration on the anticipated gain made him blind to his precarious situation.

I suddenly stopped, turned around, and for the first time in an agonizing hour looked straight at him. I had seen such faces before; they represented another ghetto, a ghetto of destitution, dire poverty, filth, and crime. They were the faces of people diseased in both mind and body who constituted the lowest denominator of a civilized society in any country, but more so in Poland, where exploitation of the people had finally been perfected after many years of occupation by three of its neighbors: Germany, Austria, and Russia. That made Poland an ideal breeding ground for young criminals such as the one I now confronted.

How could I think of attacking such a miserable creature, even in self-defense? He had never had a chance to learn what human dignity was all about. I turned away from him in disgust and decided on another plan to get rid of him. I reached my neighborhood, and he was still close behind me when I turned left toward my former residence building. The apartment house I used to live in had entrances on two streets, one on Szeroka and the other on Brukowa. I headed for the Spicmachers' apartment, which fronted on Szeroka Street. As I crossed the street in front of the King Kasimir the Great preparatory school, which was located directly across from their apartment, it was evident that the young man would not let go easily. I felt that the only way to get rid of him was for me to enter the Spicmachers' home. All that time I had not uttered a sound while he tried his best to provoke me into talking. I stopped for a second outside the apartment and asked him what he wanted.

"You know what I want!" he replied. "I know you're a Jew. You won't fool me!"

I entered the Spicmachers' apartment and found that their son, Waclaw, was home. After I told Waclaw what had happened, he went out into the street and started beating the parasite while I made my exit through the back door to Brukowa Street.

# 6 Liquidation of the Sokolow Ghetto

After spending the night with Stan and resting from the nightmare day before, I again left for Sokolow, where everything seemed to be normal.

A few days later news spread to Sokolow that the Nazis had started a mass deportation of Jews from the Warsaw ghetto to Treblinka. Smugglers who had traveled through Treblinka told us that freight trains loaded with what appeared to be Jews were passing through the Malkinia station on their way to the Treblinka camp. The trains were moving day and night without respite, and the sounds coming from the cattle cars made it clear that children were in there also.

Until then no one had the slightest idea that Treblinka was anything other than a labor camp. But most people were still naïve to the point of disbelief. "What would children do in a labor camp?" they asked. The answer came soon enough, at least for me.

A few people who managed to escape from the Warsaw ghetto to Sokolow told us that the Nazis, with the help of the Polish and ghetto police, had surrounded entire blocks and ordered every man, woman, and child to come down into the courtyard and form columns for deportation. Anyone found hiding or not moving for any reason was shot on sight. So assembled, they were marched to the railroad station and from there sent to Treblinka.

I received an appeal for help from inside Treblinka in the form of a message from my friend Dr. Mandel. He was in a barrack with a group of men selected for work because of their strong physiques. He told me that they had separated him from his wife, and he did not know what had happened to her.

Of course, I could do nothing to help him. The ghetto policeman who brought me the message said he was going back there the next day with a delivery and could take a package to Dr. Mandel. I did send him a package, but I never found out whether he received it. In the meantime I learned what was happening in the Treblinka camp: they were simply exterminating the Jews en masse.

As the mass murder of those innocent people continued, the Nazis organized a *Kulturwoche,* or week of culture, in Warsaw. What an irony that while mass extermination went on, the *Warschauer Zeitung* carried large daily headlines praising the cultural achievements of Germans in the Generalgouvernement. I could find no term adequate to describe such perfidy.

For a short time I was at a loss for what to do with myself. I felt that time was beginning to run out for us too, and I did not want to wind up in that extermination camp. I approached a few young men in the ghetto to perhaps join me in going to the nearby forests. Having heard that there were already some partisans in the area, I thought that perhaps we could make contact with them and join forces. I was sure it was better to get killed fighting than to be slaughtered like sheep. No one, however, seemed interested in going into the woods. One young man told me that his father, who was a very pious man, had a dream in which he was told that the extermination of the rest of the Jews would stop with the extermination of the Jews of the Warsaw ghetto. Thus, the Jews of Sokolow had nothing more to fear, and he could see no reason to go to the woods to fight for his life. But I grew more restless every day and kept thinking about getting out of the ghetto. I finally succeeded in organizing a group of thirty people to go, if not into the woods, then at least into the countryside, where there was a better chance of escape if need be.

On August 20, 1942, roughly one month after the beginning of the extermination of the Jews from the Warsaw ghetto, the Nazis repeated the same process in Siedlce, a town only eighteen miles south of Sokolow. These new events called for us to reconsider our situation. I was sure that we had to move out of Sokolow without delay, so I gathered my group, and we abandoned Sokolow that night for the village of Repki, located six miles away. Repki at one time had been an estate of considerable size. One of our group knew most of the farmers in the village and was on especially good terms with the largest landowner there. Joseph Kopyto had made prior arrangements with that landowner on our behalf, and so we journeyed to the Repki estate, where we were given a little abandoned house on the edge of the property, and its close proximity to a patch of forest imbued us with a sense of security.

Kopyto, who was instrumental in securing that place for us, had been a grain broker before the war and through his business connections had developed a close friendship with the owner of that estate. The landowner himself had been forced to vacate his home and turn it over fully furnished to the Nazis, who then converted it into a rehabilitation center for soldiers wounded at the Russian front. Occasionally we would see a large Red Cross vehicle drive up to the main house and unload stretchers holding the wounded men.

Somehow being close to Mother Nature made the group feel more at ease. After settling down in Repki, we agreed to pay for the hospitality with work in the fields. It was harvest time, and there was plenty of work for everyone. My first job was in the blacksmith shop, and later I too worked the fields, driving a diesel tractor to plow and do other types of work. We bought food from the small farms nearby and left one of the group, a girl, in the house to prepare food for us. We were organized almost like a kibbutz in Palestine. The Germans in Repki ignored us, and we were very careful not to change that situation.

Work in the fields was rather pleasant, and time passed much more quickly than before. Life might have been considered tolerable had the constant danger not been present and had one's mind not been burdened with recent nightmarish experiences. Once in a while the calm was interrupted by machine-gun fire—a refreshing indication that partisans were active in the area.

Luckily food was not a problem, since there were plenty of potatoes on hand, and we had the money to pay for them. We ate potatoes three times a day, seven days a week, and seemed not to tire of them.

I did, however, have an unpleasant experience in Repki when I was working in the blacksmith shop with a father and his son, who were both Catholic. Refugees from the Polish province of Poznan, they ended up working at the estate after the Nazis took their home and large farm and shipped them off to the Generalgouvernement. On several occasions the son asked me to give him my suit. At that time I had only one suit and an extra pair of trousers, and I frankly did not like such rudeness. I remained noncommittal. One day that boy sneeringly blurted out, "After all, you will not have the opportunity much longer to wear that suit, since the Nazis are going to take you to Treblinka anyway. What you are doing is only stupid Jewish stubbornness." Fortunately, nothing more came of it.

With the approach of the high holy days of Yom Kippur, some of our group wanted to go to town, since we had no provision for conducting religious services at the house. Even in town the facilities were clandestine; from the very beginning the Nazis had prohibited Jews from assembling for any purpose, including religious services. So four men from our group, including Kopyto's father-in-law, went to Sokolow that day to pray, believing, presumably, that prayer in a formal congregation was bound to have better results with Almighty God. I tried to persuade them not to go, but I finally gave up because, as a rule, it is folly to argue with anyone on religious matters.

The following day, Yom Kippur, we were given a day off from work in recognition of the holy day. It probably would have been better to have kept working, since nobody had any desire to pray openly, although we did pray silently. Full of bitterness and resentment rather than humility, our state of mind was not conducive to prayer, at least not the way prayers are said in a temple. Once in a while someone in the group would attempt to start a conversation, but it usually was of no avail.

The four men did not come back Yom Kippur Day as we had expected, generating concern among us for their safety. Then, after night fell, a man wearing a Polish army coat arrived at our house, and what he had to tell us was simply incredible. I recognized him from a brief conversation we'd once had in the Sokolow ghetto; only now did I find out that his name was Leon Peregal. He also remembered me from the ghetto, but likewise he did not know my name.

He told us that at four o'clock that morning he'd been awakened by a neighbor yelling, "The Hell's Fire Devils are here!" He jumped out of bed, got dressed and went out into the street, where men, women, and children were running for their lives, searching for cover from bullets being sprayed in all directions from outside the ghetto by black-uniformed Lithuanians and Ukrainians. He joined a group of people marching toward the Judenrat office, but then he separated from the group and began looking for a way out. Making an on-the-spot decision, he quickly scaled an eight-foot-high wooden fence, topped with barbed wire, that separated the ghetto from a lumberyard he had visited several times before when painting signs for the owner, a Polish merchant named Yankowski. As he jumped down into the lumber yard, he was immediately attacked by two German shepherd dogs, but the younger dog—a six-month-old puppy that Leon had played with during his previous visits—recognized him and held the other at bay.

Leon broke into the office and stayed there for a while, but then he went back into the yard and looked into the ghetto through cracks in the fence. He couldn't believe his eyes. He saw black-uniformed Lithuanians dragging Jews outside, shooting anyone who made a wrong move. He even saw one of the murderers holding a baby by its feet and smashing its head against the wall. Dead bodies littered the ground.

Returning to the office, he waited there until that afternoon, when he heard Polish children in the street outside the ghetto happily yelling that the last of the Jews were being led out of the ghetto. Still later a Polish man unlocked the main door to the yard and came in to feed the dogs. It was someone whom Leon knew and felt he could trust, so he made his presence known to him. The man told Leon that now nobody was out in the street and it would be safe for him to leave. So Leon emerged slowly, not looking back, and walked away. He walked on the highway for several miles until a peasant came up behind him and gave him a ride in his horse-drawn wagon. He started telling Leon that horrible things were going on in the city, that they were shooting the Jews and loading them into cattle cars at the train station. He suspected that Leon was Jewish and told him that he worked at the Repki estate where many Jews from Sokolow were working, and that Leon could join them if he wanted. It was dark when they got to the estate, and the driver showed Leon the way to the house where we were hiding.

Over the next several days, news filtered in from others who had escaped, including one of the Jewish policemen from the ghetto. A picture of what had happened began to emerge. There had been approximately seven thousand Jews living in Sokolow, and in only one day the Nazis managed to remove almost all the ghetto population from the town. In their insane action to eradicate everything Jewish, on Yom Kippur eve the Nazis had surrounded the entire Sokolow ghetto with German and Polish police forces and some SD men as well. The SS men and the black-uniformed SD troops went into the ghetto in the early morning hours and set up a loudspeaker that blared out an order for the Jews to assemble in front of the Judenrat office. Once at the assembly place, the Jews were put into groups that were marched off in military order to the railroad station, where they were locked up in awaiting cattle cars. When no more volunteers were forthcoming, the Nazis began a search-and-destroy operation through the houses, killing everyone they found. Still later the assassins went from house to house, tapping the floors and walls with metal rods and listening for hollow sounds that would indicate the presence of hiding places. When one was found, the Nazis would break through and pull out the Jews who were hiding there. All the hidden Jews—men, women, and children—were brought to the yard in front of the synagogue, where the young men were ordered to dig a large grave. All the victims were put at the edge of the mass grave and shot, so that their bodies fell on top of one another. The Nazis then made the president of the Sokolow Judenrat go down into the grave and stand on top of the bodies while one of the SS men took his picture. Then they shot him dead.

Those events in Sokolow created a panic in our camp. I went to work as usual, but my mind was not able to concentrate on the job. I had to figure out what to do next. The immediate decision I made was to move out of the house that I shared with the rest of the group. I decided to sleep in the field in a large haystack so that I would not be caught by surprise. My son, Samuel, was with me at the time. Every night both of us walked about one mile from the house to the haystack and buried ourselves in it to sleep.

Meanwhile we learned that a mass murder had occurred in Kossow only one day after the Sokolow catastrophe, and I immediately sent a farmer friend there with a letter in the hope that my mother and brother were still alive. Fortunately they were among the few who were spared, but my brother, Leon, had lost his wife and little girl to the Nazi assassins. Leon informed me in his message that the Nazis had murdered only part of the Jewish population in Kossow. According to my brother, the Nazis deported most of the Kossow Jews to the nearby Treblinka death camp. Others were assembled, marched to the nearby Jewish cemetery almost two miles away, made dig their own graves, and shot so that they fell in. Slave laborers then were made to cover up the bodies. The next day my brother and a few other men went to the cemetery and found some of those victims still breathing, but they could do nothing to help.

After the deportation and mass murder, a German named von Eupen, who was head of the SS at Treblinka, assured the surviving Jews in Kossow that he had received an order not to molest them, and from that point on there would be no more killings. My brother, who was then a Jewish police-man, suggested that I should send my son to stay with him and my mother, since the child would be much safer with them. I found my brother's reasoning convincing, and I knew that my mother wanted Samuel there with her. So I paid a Polish farmer a huge sum of money to take my son to them in Kossow. And suddenly I was alone.

# 7 Twice Saved by Intuition

There was more news from Sokolow. The Nazis apparently had found a few additional Jews hiding in the ghetto and had started another terror search that turned up even more. Some had even been found hiding inside bakery ovens. We knew it was only a matter of days before we would be next on the murderers' list, and it was therefore imperative to make a decision. I thought of moving on right away.

But it was Leon Peregal who spoke up first this time. He usually was soft-spoken, but now even he felt the urgency of the hour. He suggested that we start immediately on our way to a safer place. We started by changing our appearances. Leon managed to alter his beyond recognition with just a change of a garment and cap. Now he looked like a real back-country peasant.

I received unexpected help from a lady storekeeper in the village, a displaced Russian from Bialystok who, by her own experience, was aware of our predicament. Her help to me came in the form of a document without which it was impossible to go anywhere in Poland. She had found an identity card lost in her store by a local drunkard and had kept it believing it might be of use to me. She also gave her brother's card to Leon. If Leon had not been a photographer and artist, those cards would have been of little use to us. But with his talent, they were just what we needed. We had a camera to make our own snapshots, and Leon did a masterful job of filling in the balance of the official stamp, part of which had been removed with the old picture. Another lady gave us the address of a place near the Slovakian border. She thought that the little hamlet of Busko would be the safest place for us to stay.

Before going to Busko I decided to see my family first. We made the sixteen miles from Repki to the vicinity of Kossow in about six hours going across fields and avoiding any roads. We stopped at a friend's farm in Cholidow because I could not enter Kossow for security reasons. My friend Mr. Zielinski brought my family to me, and we spent a while together. My brother claimed to feel secure where he was, saying that he had enough friends among local farmers to find refuge when and if necessary.

We left the Zielinski place late that night and took a train from Lacki toward the general direction of Busko. We had with us a letter of recommendation from that fine lady in Repki to present to the owner of an estate in Busko.

Arriving at Busko two days later, we were the only passengers who got off the train there. The stationmaster showed us the road to the Busko estate and told us the distance was about two miles. For some reason we became suspicious as we approached the place. With less than a half-mile to go, we started hearing a familiar melody. It was the melody of a Nazi song. That was sufficient reason for us to turn around and move away as quickly as possible.

It was already quite late in the evening, and wandering at night in German-occupied territory was in itself a dangerous undertaking. We noticed a small farmhouse by the side of the road and decided to approach the farmer to ask for information about the Busko estate. I knocked at their door. I do not believe there can be any more difficult way to make friends with a stranger than to awaken him in the process, but luck was with us. The farmer expressed delight in seeing that we were not Germans, asked us into his modest home, and prepared a kettle of tea. He then proceeded to tell us the story of the Busko estate.

Several months before, the Nazis had discovered a lack of loyalty on the part of the estate management. In a carbon-copy repetition of their actions all over Poland and other occupied countries in Europe, the Nazis came in force, took the owner and managers to a concentration camp, and assumed complete control. Only weeks before our arrival, the Nazis had brought slave laborers in to build barracks for what had become a Hitler Jugend camp. That explained why we had heard the Nazi song that evening.

This information caused us to change our plans again. I asked the farmer permission to stay there overnight, and he gave his consent with pleasure. We now faced the question of where to go next, but that problem solved itself rather easily. When the farmer mentioned that he had to deliver potatoes in the morning to the train bound for Deblin, Leon and I both, without giving it a second thought, exclaimed together, "Let's go to Deblin!"

The failure of our plans had us bordering on frustration, but we were not yet to the point of desperation; neither of us had lost hope. We rested in the barn for a few hours on the warm, fragrant hay.

Early the next morning, the farmer's wife asked us into the house to join them for breakfast, which consisted of simple potato soup flavored with milk and a piece of black bread. After that healthy meal, Leon and I went to the railroad station with our friend the farmer.

The station was a typical Austro-Hungarian-type structure, usually put up in small places. (Actually, to apply the term *station* to that little place, with the imposing name of "Busko," would be an exaggeration; *railroad stop* would be a better term.) It consisted of a rectangular building approximately twelve by fourteen feet in size. The manager's office and ticket desk were at one end, and the remainder was a waiting room with a large pot-bellied coal-burning stove. Smoke and draft pipes ran in zigzags throughout the room to give the maximum distribution of heat. Despite the warm comfort inside, reasons of safety made the outside chill more inviting to us. Viewed against the tragic events of the recent past, our survival required that we be alert to possible surprises. It was necessary for us to see ahead as far as possible to ensure sufficient time to make the proper decisions. We therefore waited outside until it was time to buy the tickets and board the train.

Exactly why we should, or perhaps should not, go to Deblin, I couldn't explain. As time passed, however, for some unknown reason, Deblin began to move out of my mind, and we decided against going there. As we faced the tracks, the train going to Deblin should have come from the left, a northeasterly direction. But the train was overdue and another was approaching from the right, coming from the direction of Deblin itself. Turning progressively more nervous as fear slowly overcame us, we walked into the station and noticed that the destination of the train just arriving was Lukow, a town in the opposite direction from Deblin. I bought tickets for Lukow.

All that happened mechanically. Deblin. Lukow. Those were abstract terms to us and nothing more. All we were looking for was a spot on earth where we could live in peace and safety. It was like a bad dream. Leon was sick with tuberculosis, and my problem was a neck swollen from an infection. The deficiencies we experienced were obviously the result of an abnormal way of living, which excluded the most elemental needs of a sanitary life. Literally like hunted animals, we were under constant stress.

Once on the train, we took our seats in what we thought was an empty compartment. As it turned out, a couple of passengers had left the compartment for a stroll in the corridor. They returned when the train started moving and sat down after giving us a friendly greeting. We developed a congenial conversation with them and thus learned some important news that was of special concern to us. The two passengers told us that the night before, the Gestapo and SD had surrounded the station in Deblin and hauled all the non-German passengers away in trucks. Those who tried to escape were shot to death. Our fellow travelers had saved themselves by walking seven miles at night to wait for this train. We listened attentively, thinking to ourselves what could have happened had we stayed with our original plan.

I kept wondering what had made me change destinations in Busko without even attempting to discuss it with Leon. I had acted almost mechanically, as if in a trance, and could find no logical explanation for my actions. It turned out to be the right decision in the light of subsequent events. Leon tried to explain it as intuition; perhaps he was right. Sometimes decisions made on the spur of the moment were more productive than those resulting from long and careful planning.

With the monotonous tick-and-tack of the wheels on the loose rails, I was turning ideas over in my mind more quickly than the train was moving. The main problem was to unearth a formula for survival, and there I had to admit defeat. Unable to find a set rule to follow safely, I came to the inescapable conclusion that the only thing to do was to continue with my ad hoc improvisations. I was so deep in thought that I hardly noticed that our compartment was periodically filling with more passengers. My movements to make room on the bench for more people were mechanical. It was a long way to Lukow.

We were finally approaching the town late in the afternoon when the train suddenly stopped. I looked out the window and noticed that we were in a field in the middle of nowhere. The station was apparently still far away. Through the car window on the opposite side I could see a red signal, indicating that the train had no clearance from the station. Usually such stoppages were of short duration.

We were still sitting there after almost one hour, with no change in sight. As a rule, such a prolonged stay would produce a feeling of insecurity, particularly in an unknown place, so I decided to step out and look around. There was snow on the ground, and the sun was close to the horizon. I noticed a road on the left running parallel to the railroad track, and I called Leon out of the car. We walked across the field to the road and then followed the road toward town. We did not know the distance to Lukow, but that was of little significance. On our way we passed a small coffee shop on the left and several houses scattered along the road.

Soon we noticed some men running in our direction. We stopped at first, but as they came closer, we turned back and headed for the coffee shop. There we stopped again and waited. As they approached, we saw them to be civilians and asked them why they were running. Petrified, they could hardly breathe from running. After a long pause, they told us the reason for their fear. What happened in Deblin the night before had happened in Lukow during the daytime, and—as far as we could determine—was still in progress. That of course eliminated Lukow as a harbor for us. In the coffee shop we found out that several months earlier the Nazis had killed all the Jews in Lukow in a single day.

We asked for a cup of tea and for information concerning the train schedules. One particular place appealed to me more than others, but for no special reason. The town was Terespol, located on the Bug River, directly opposite Brest Litovsk. Terespol had previously been a border town on the demarcation line between the German- and Russian-occupied territories, and it still served as a border town separating the Generalgouvernement from the territory taken from the Soviets.

Later that evening news was brought from Lukow that all was clear. The Nazis, we were told, had hauled away a dozen large truckloads of men, women, and children.

Twice in only twenty-four hours I had the unusual experience of instinctive forewarning of danger to us both. I told Leon that a strange feeling of restlessness had overcome me and made me act as I had. He speculated that it was best explained as extrasensory perception.

Leon and I worked out a plan in case we got separated. We agreed to contact each other through two different channels. One was by way of my friend Stanislaw in Praga, and the other was by way of Mr. Zielinski in Kossow. Those two families in turn had each other's address.

On the train to Terespol we met a nice young man who gave us some information about the town. The Nazis, he said, had already solved the Jewish problem there by killing all the Jews. He told us that he had only recently settled in Terespol, having been originally from Lodz. There was something about him that generated trust and confidence, and I actually enjoyed the conversation with him. When we got to Terespol, he took us to a coffee shop that he owned and introduced us to his wife and son, and we shared their family dinner.

Since Terespol was a small town, I thought it would be hard for both Leon and me to circulate inconspicuously. I therefore decided to leave Leon there and go on to Warsaw. We had learned from our railroad acquaintance that the German border command always needed men to work locally, so we planned for Leon to obtain a job and then notify me through our established channels to come join him.

After midnight I left on the next train and arrived in Praga that afternoon. I first went to the closest place I could think of in the vicinity of the railroad station. The Wozniak family and I had been friends and neighbors for many years, but they had not seen me since the beginning of the war. Although they seemed happy to see me, I thought I detected fear in their faces, fear that they tried in vain to hide. I, of course, was not interested in jeopardizing their safety, so I notified my friend Stan, who promptly came to get me.

Stanislaw Gorczyca lived in the Wawer section of Praga. His small brick house was in a secluded spot next to a dense patch of forest where one could hide if needed. But the house alone, and the favorable conditions surrounding it, would not have been enough to inspire me with hope and confidence had it not been for Stan's gracious hospitality. He offered me not only shelter but friendship. Stan was an employee of the post office, and it was well known that those particular government workers were not paid much. Yet he was quick to tell me: "If you don't have any money, don't you worry. Only you will have to be satisfied with whatever my wife can put on the table for my family, and that includes you."

Stan's only neighbor was a Volksdeutscher, but my experience with my former landlord, Wilhelm Spicmacher, had shown me that not all Volksdeutsche were bad news. The difference here was that I did not know Stan's neighbor, and Stan had not lived there long enough to make friends with him. For the time being, I did not worry too much about it.

Stan introduced me to his wife and his two little boys as his cousin on his mother's side (the arm of the family with which they were not familiar). According to my new identity card, which Stan obtained from the Polish underground, my name, too, was Stanislaw, since we both supposedly had been named after the same ancestor. The boys called me Uncle Stan.

In such a favorable family environment, life had a tendency to approach normalcy. My nerves began to relax after several days of calm, and with my return to quasi-normal life, concern for my family grew. I began to think that perhaps I could include my son in our group. Stan's boys were older than my Samuel, but I decided to ask Stan what he thought of the idea. Without hesitation, he agreed that it would be not only possible but also rather desirable, and he suggested that we both go to Kossow to get my son. This gesture of his was more than just noble; it was altruism at its fullest.

At the end of November 1942, Stan took a few days' leave from his job, and we left together by train for Kossow. Stan gave me his postman's uniform, and he wore my civilian clothes.

At eleven o'clock in the evening we got to Malkinia, where we had to change trains. I was on familiar ground in Malkinia, but this time the train normally waiting to take off for Kossow was not there. It was not safe to wait in Malkinia, so Stan and I, as well as a few smugglers, decided to walk to Kossow. About a mile from Malkinia was the Bug River and a bridge for us to cross. On the other side, a mile or so past the bridge and hidden in the woods, was the infamous Treblinka extermination camp. There was a good road paralleling the railroad track, but it was covered with snow. For a certain distance we were able to follow the track, which was partly clear because of the heavy traffic to and from the death camp.

The moon in all its majesty had turned the night almost into daylight, so the soldier at the bridge had no problem noticing us at a fair distance. As we came closer, he yelled to us in German to halt. I answered him in German, asking him to let us pass and explaining that we were on our way to Kossow. Hearing my clear German and noticing the outline of my uniform, he took me for some kind of officer and waved us on. When we approached the station at Treblinka, we realized why there had been no train from Malkinia. Both tracks at the Treblinka station and far beyond it were filled with freight trains waiting to be admitted to the slaughterhouse.

We got off the tracks and took to the road that ran parallel, keeping approximately thirty feet from the trains. We walked in agony for what seemed like an eternity, to the accompaniment of children's cries and the quiet whining of elders, to the lamentations and loud prayers to God, a God who did not seem to hear their pleas for recourse. Others begged for water in different languages. I understood them all.

None of us uttered a sound.

The trains were guarded by surprisingly few men walking up and down the tracks. To me those guards looked like former Soviet prisoners of war from the Ukraine, Latvia, and Lithuania who now wore the black SD uniform. I noticed that each train ended with a passenger car that housed the SS men who commanded the guards.

While walking along the road past that Moloch, witnessing humanity's cruelty to its own kind, I glanced at Stan. He was crying. So was I. Even those otherwise hard-boiled smugglers kept drying their eyes.

What seemed like an eternity came to a sudden end at the two-kilometer marker, where the railroad track turned to the right and entered a patch of dense woods. The camp was approximately one mile away from that point. After unloading the human cargo, the Nazis routed the trains through Siedlce for refill rather than go back to Malkinia. This apparently was done to keep the trains moving efficiently and provide for one-way traffic only.

About halfway on the road between Malkinia and Kossow, we came to a point within a half-mile from the camp. It was then that we detected the odor of burning flesh. The closer we got, the more intense the odor became, until the air was full of the sweet smell of roasted meat. According to information we received from farmers in the surrounding area, as well as from Ukrainian guards who had escaped from the camp, the Nazis at Treblinka subjected their victims first to poison gas and then subsequently burned their corpses in open ditches dug especially for that purpose. Digging in the camp presented no problem, since that area was a large sand pit dating back to the building of the railroad in that part of the country. Covering up the ignoble effort of twentieth-century German culture was an equally easy job, because of the sandy terrain.

After reaching some distance from that hell, we looked back and noticed a reflection in the sky from the flaming ditches. We walked all the faster to get away from it as quickly as possible, never speaking a word until we part-ed company with the smugglers. The experience was too grave, the depress-ing mood it created too deep, to be disturbed with idle talk.

On the road we were passed by a passenger car containing SS men fol-lowed by two trucks loaded with SD troops. They were coming from the di-rection of Treblinka on their way to some settlement to solve the Jewish ques-tion the Hitler way, by murdering the men, young and old; the women, sick or healthy; and the innocent children—all for the glory of the projected thou-sand-year Reich.

We reached Kossow at about one o'clock in the morning and immedi-ately departed for the station with my son. I could not permit myself to be seen in Kossow at all, much less in a uniform. That would have cost Stan's life as well as my own. We could not afford to wait in Kossow until daylight, so we climbed on the first freight train that came along to get to Siedlce, where we could catch a passenger train to Warsaw. That evening we were back in Stan's house in Wawer, this time in company with my son, and everything seemed to be just fine.

Although I watched Samuel so that he would not be conspicuous in the neighborhood, it was hard to keep an eight-year-old boy confined in a house. He would go out to play with Stan's boys, who were much older and larger than he. I noticed other people beginning to show an interest in him. Peri-odically they would talk to him and ask him different questions. I became suspicious and had a feeling that Stan's wife was asking questions, too. I shared my concern with Stan and found out that I was unfortunately right— the neighbors were asking Stan questions he could not answer. I was aware that I was exposing my friends to danger, that their house could be burned down and the whole Gorczyca family shot on account of me. That was too great a sacrifice to demand, even from the best of friends. I asked Stan to take my son back to my mother and brother in Kossow.*

---

*Editor's note: My father left approximately six weeks of time unaccounted for between this sen-tence and the next both in his original memoir written in Polish and in its English translation. He rarely spoke to us, his second family, about this time period, and out of respect for his wishes, we never questioned him about it. We do know that he returned to Kossow and brought his son to a Gentile friend, a farmer (Zielinski?) who hid the boy in his home. In the process of getting Samuel out of Kossow, my father was shot in the right leg; he stayed in the farmer's barn until he recovered enough to return to Warsaw. In his absence, his brother, thinking Samuel would be safer with him, brought the boy back to Kossow, and soon thereafter Samuel, his uncle, and his grandmother were taken to Treblinka and put to death.

Adversities usually appear in the least opportune times, and so it was with me. I contracted a bad cold while still suffering from a wounded leg, and in such a condition I could not impose myself on those wonderful people any longer.

With my fever having passed, although my leg was still swollen, I decided to leave Stan's house for another place in the opposite part of the city, a one-room apartment in the suburb of Wola that was occupied by Frank, a mutual friend of Stan and myself. Frank was a bachelor living at 18 Mlynarska Street. He, like Stan, was happy to share his modest abode with me. The first thing I had to do was to get a doctor to treat the gangrene in my leg, and the neighbors across the hall helped me with this. That same evening I was received by their cousin, a doctor who took care of my injury and infection. As it turned out, that injured leg would play a major role in saving my life.

Periodically the Nazis went on hunting sprees, which they called *Razzien* (police raids), to catch men and women for slave labor in German factories. They usually cordoned off an entire area, blocked off several streets, and methodically went from building to building, from apartment to apartment, forcing everybody down to the street and into big military trucks. The victims were then taken to the railroad station and from there sent to Germany. Several *Razzien* had taken place recently in Warsaw, supposedly in retaliation for acts of sabotage committed in the area. On January 15, 1943, the Nazis organized such a hunt in the western section of Warsaw, and since the Wola suburb was part of that section, I was right in the path of the *Razzia*.

The lady from across the hall knocked on my door and told me what was going on; she knew because her apartment faced the front toward the street, but Frank's was to the rear, so that I could neither see nor hear any of it. I left the room, locking it behind me, and entered the woman's apartment. I looked through her window but could see nothing except people running in panic. A short time later we saw the first green-uniformed Nazi policeman entering the courtyard. He waited until more policemen came, and then groups of five entered different stairwells. I had a quick idea to let the woman lock me up in my apartment, but I was simply unable to get it unlocked, so we quickly returned to her apartment. I sat down in a chair with my injured leg on another and waited for them to come in. The lady grabbed her little child and waited also. She was as white as freshly fallen snow. Only seconds passed from when I sat down until they broke in the door, but for us it seemed a lifetime.

The leader of the group, a sergeant, walked into the room with one other man while the rest stayed in the hall. I don't know how to explain it, but the instant I saw their faces, I became calm. Perhaps it was a natural sense of resignation that overcomes a person in the face of extreme adversity, since all I could expect was death. Or perhaps it was a feeling of being alone, of losing hope, or of having passed the hour of salvation. Whatever it was, I had no more fear. I looked straight into their faces and waited for the command to get up and go down with them into the street.

Instead, the sergeant asked me in German what I was doing at home. According to my identity card, I was supposed to be a country yokel, so I pretended that I did not understand what he was saying. He repeated the question and still got no reply. He happened to have one Polish-speaking Nazi with him, whom he ordered to ask the same question in Polish. I readily showed him my identity card and my swollen, bloody leg while explaining that the leg was the reason I was at home that time of day.

They hung around for a few seconds, looking at me again and then at the woman with the child. Then they turned and left the room without closing the door. After breaking down the door to my room and finding it empty, they finally left for good. That day the Nazis arrested about fifty men and women in our building alone.

I collapsed and could not move a muscle for quite a while. That was the closest face-to-face encounter with disaster I had experienced thus far in my life. But it was only a temporary reaction to the terrible strain on my nervous system. The poor woman told me afterward that she thought I was dying and handed me a little alcohol, which helped put me back in order again. The pressure on me was so great that I was certain that if I lived through all this, I would surely drop dead afterward like some overripe fruit.

# 8 Escape to Berlin

I received a letter from Leon Peregal shortly after my encounter with the Nazi sergeant. Leon informed me that he had landed a job in Terespol as a painter with the border-patrol unit, known as the Grenzschutz. Later I found out that Leon's job was to paint pictures of the wives or mistresses of the Nazi officers. Leon asked me to come to Terespol as quickly as possible, certain that I could get a job there too. Disregarding my sore leg, which had not quite healed, I decided to go to Terespol. I informed Stan of my decision, and he offered me his uniform again, saying that if I did not like it in Terespol, the uniform would facilitate my return to Warsaw. Once again I went traveling dressed as a postal worker.

Terespol was a typical old Russian town with buildings of wooden construction, except for the railroad station, which was built of masonry. Indicative of modern times were the crosses placed in the windows or above the doors of some houses, precautions taken by the non-Jewish population in hopes that the Nazi assassins would bypass their homes during the massacres of the Jews. Since Terespol had been a largely Jewish town, bypassing a few houses presented no major problem for the Hitlerite murderers. Other houses, by far the great majority, had no signs at all; these houses were empty.

Finding Leon's workplace was easy, because that camp was the only one in the area and was visible from anywhere in town. Leon introduced me to the camp commander after we had a short conference together. Leon told him that I was a cousin from Warsaw who was trying to get away from a nagging wife for a while and that I was going far enough away from the city and my family to have some peace at last.

The commander had a big laugh at my miserable condition, but he then showed a great understanding of my situation and immediately offered me a job. He promised that if my wife showed up at his camp to take me back home, he would see to it that she would never find me. I in turn expressed appreciation for his generosity and man-to-man understanding. I told him that I would have to go back to Warsaw to get an indefinite leave of absence from my job at the post office. "After all," I explained, "this is a government job, and I feel it is my duty. I will be back after a couple of days to start my new job here." That same day Leon introduced me to his landlady, who agreed to set one more bed in Leon's room for an additional consideration.

Early the following morning I was back on my way to Warsaw with a few snapshots of Leon and myself for use in preparing new identity cards. On my way back I had to change trains in Siedlce, since the train I was on had an East Prussian destination. I spent my time walking around outside on the platform while waiting for the train to Warsaw.

While I was waiting, I entered the public latrine, and as I was walking out, a man with what I thought was a familiar face passed me on his way in. It took me only a few seconds to recognize that short, stocky fellow, but my postal uniform and short beard probably slowed his recognition of me. He could not immediately make up his mind as to my identity, and that short interval of indecision gave me the time I needed to put some distance between us.

About a year or so before, I had sold him a bicycle in Kossow. After he had used it for a few months, he looked me up and asked me to swap it for a brand new one, without any additional expense to him. I would not agree, and that was the last time I had seen him—until now. His unusual attempt to get something in an unfair manner impressed me so much that his facial characteristics remained deeply etched in my mind. Because he failed to get his way, he evidently remembered my face as well.

I turned to the right and away from the station at a fast pace. Because the station serviced trains on both sides, to leave it one had to cross a major set of railroad tracks. A train was coming, and as I moved rapidly through the crossing, I had just enough time to give a fleeting glance behind me. He was after me, all right. I increased my speed until I was almost running and made it across just in time, putting that train between me and my pursuer.

There was a coffee shop about half a block past the crossing on the left. As far as I could see, there was nowhere else to take refuge, and time was short. The train was almost through the crossing, and I would be trapped if I could find no way out of the dilemma. I could expect a classic repetition of so many other tragedies: first blackmail, then robbery, and finally being turned over to the Nazis.

Just before the train cleared the crossing, I walked into the coffee shop and positioned myself behind a cabinet on the far end of the counter where the owner kept his cake and cookies. The top of the cabinet was approximately six feet high, and since I stand five feet, seven inches, I was well hidden once I took off my hat. From my position I could see what was happening on the street in front of the shop.

I did not have to wait long. There he was with another, taller fellow, at first bypassing the coffee shop. Then they returned and went the other way, but they came back again. I asked for a cup of tea, and the lady handed it to me where I was, while I kept the front under constant observation. My pursuers stopped in front of the shop and looked into the display window for a few minutes. The shorter one opened the door and looked around for a minute. Then he closed the door, and they both walked away—but returned again! I had not moved from my spot. I couldn't tell what they were saying to each other, but I saw them shake their heads in disbelief. Once again the short one opened the door, looked around, and closed it.

To them it must have seemed like I had disappeared into thin air. The reason they did not walk into the coffee shop was that two Germans were sitting at a table in the middle of the room. Whenever the door was opened, one of the Germans would turn his head to see who it was, as if he was expecting someone. I believe this circumstance saved the day for me.

A glance at my watch told me that my pursuer had only ten minutes left before his train departure. I, of course, knew where he was going and that the next train in his direction would not be until the same time the following day. Such a fellow could ill afford to remain here one more day. The way things had turned out for him, he probably was less sure of himself now than he had been only minutes before; nevertheless, I kept up my alertness. Ten minutes after they had gone, I heard the long whistle of the departing train, and I was sure that my pursuer had taken the train home. He was, after all, a farmer. I waited a little longer and then went outside, proceeding slowly to the station. After a while my train pulled in, and I took a seat in a car full of noisy women smugglers.

During the latest incident I had the feeling of being cornered between a hyena and a vulture. It created in me a sense of utter disgust in some elements of the human race, and it fortified my determination to fight to the last. It also taught me a very important lesson. I now was aware that a uniform and a beard alone did not necessarily transform me beyond recognition, and I knew I would have to be more careful in the future. I also decided never again to take advantage of Stan's generosity concerning the uniform.

Back in Warsaw I related my recent experiences to Stan, and he secured two new identify cards from the Polish underground for Leon and myself. I then returned to Terespol to assume my job with the Greenshirts alongside Leon. My acceptance there was a foregone conclusion, and my activities were diverse. I was an electrician, an automobile mechanic, and an authority in the different phases of design, construction, and assembly of prefabricated units. Anyone with a little ingenuity could have done the same thing, perhaps better, but apparently it was in my destiny to be the expert.

The apartment we occupied was fine, but we had to stay on our toes to keep from being detected. Each morning we got up early and knelt before our beds, crossed ourselves, and then prayed to some kind of religious image on the wall. This was for the benefit of our landlady and her children.

One day the son of the man we had met and befriended when we first arrived in Terespol, who also worked in the camp, overheard a conversation in which some workers claimed that a boy working with a crew of carpenters was a Jew. Others in that group thought it was simply impossible. Our friend's son related the conversation to Leon, who soon located the Jewish boy and managed to warn him. The boy told Leon that he was originally from Lublin, a city in central Poland, and had recently escaped from a nearby slave labor camp. Leon provided him with food and directions that he hoped would lead him to the Russian partisans and wished him well as he left the camp.

As it turned out, Leon's warning did save that young man's life. One of the workers, a man named Buzenski, was furious when he found out that he was gone. Now Buzenski was sure that the young man was a Jew, and he was angered that he so foolishly let his prey escape. He sensed treason in the camp and from that day on looked at everyone with suspicion.

Apparently one rotten apple finds its way into almost every basket. Such was the case with Buzenski. He was from the former Polish territory of Pomorze, which the Germans called "Pommern." From him we had the opportunity to learn the difference between a German by birth and one by choice. Normally he would have been just another Polish refugee, but evidently he had collaborated with the Germans even before the war. In appreciation for services rendered, they gave him a place in the Nazi Valhalla by conveniently discovering that he had a German ancestor. I was aware that people sometimes prostitute themselves to preserve a heritage, but I was at a loss to understand it from an individual of the caliber of the Buzenski fellow. By his own admission, he had been a semi-illiterate farm worker who never had anything of value in his life. After the incident with the young man, it seemed that Buzenski was constantly watching us. When I was in one room, he was in the next, always whispering so that I could not hear the conversation.

One Friday we noticed a local Gestapo man walk into the main office building. After a while he came out with Buzenski—reason enough to leave that place as soon as possible. On Saturday we requested permission to attend the early morning mass the next day, and permission was granted, provided that we reported back to work at eight o'clock that morning.

Sunday morning we got up very early and in a roundabout way left Terespol and Buzenski behind as we went out into the unknown once again. We walked through fields and woods to the next railroad station on the way to Warsaw. Two hours of fast walking carried us to a little rail stop, and before eight o'clock in the morning we were on a train to Warsaw.

One had to be lucky in those days to go anywhere and arrive at one's destination without incident. It was the beginning of 1943, and the Nazis had a valid reason to be nervous; the more intelligent Germans already knew that the war was lost. The labor shortage in Germany was acute, and the normal recruitment of men was insufficient. The Nazis thus resorted, with ever-increasing effort, to hunting at random for people to be shipped to the German industrial plants. What better way was there than to surround an incoming train, remove all the passengers, load them into trucks, haul them to a camp, and then send them to Germany? People were in constant danger of being caught this way and turned into slaves. For us the danger was twofold, since we could also be detected as Jews. This would have meant the end of our lives through cruel and agonizing torture.

About midway between Terespol and Lukow, our train stopped to let an incoming train through on the single track. As the other train slowed down, people yelled to us through the windows that the station at Lukow was surrounded and that the Germans had taken some people away. Again, the Nazis were on their usual hunting expedition. There was one more stop between us and Lukow, giving me time to think about what to do next. I came up with three possibilities: I could jump off the train and possibly get killed (or worse, only injured and then fall into the Nazis' hands incapacitated); I could sit calmly in the car until we arrived at Lukow, let the Nazis get me, and try to get away later; or I could use my main asset, the German language, and try to get away with it. This was an important decision for me, and I decided on the third course of action.

I had never been too generous with time. The time element was always an important factor with me. I had no special reason to be in a hurry, but by and large I was always moving fast, always thinking of the German saying "Morgen Morgen nur nicht heute sagen alle faule Leute" (Tomorrow, tomorrow but not today, do all the lazy people say). I lived under the constant impression that if I slowed down, I would lose the thread of events and never catch up again. That was my reason to risk the third alternative. A risk it certainly was, with an immediate climax should I fail to succeed.

At the next and last stop before Lukow, I walked out of the car and called Leon to follow me. In the center of the train were two cars reserved for Germans, and without hesitation I entered one of those cars. There were two civilians and two military men in that compartment. I greeted those present with a religious "Heil" as we made ourselves comfortable. Since Leon's German was not quite as good as mine, I did the talking. Leon remained silent, pretending he had a toothache. I always carried a bottle of vodka with me, and that day was no exception. Although I was by no means a heavy drinker, it was helpful sometimes as a tranquilizer when the excitement was excessive. I took out the bottle and offered the military men a drink after having one myself. They readily accepted. The two civilians indicated they too would like a drink, so I let them have one also. The bottle went around twice, and I left it on the bench since there was little left over. The train pulled into the station at Lukow while we were carrying on a loud and lively conversation. For the first time I had the opportunity to witness a Nazi *Razzia* taking place at a train station.

There were green-uniformed police waiting on both sides of the train, allowing no place to escape. As soon as the train stopped, a large loudspeaker issued orders, first in German and then in Polish. In Polish they told the passengers, regardless of their respective destinations, to leave the train immediately, take all their luggage with them, leave the doors wide open, and proceed to the main waiting room in the station proper. They warned that all who did not follow orders would be shot to death on the spot. The message in German had been different, however. The passengers were told not to leave their cars, to keep their doors locked, and not to let anyone in.

The whole operation took not much longer than a half an hour. The police worked with methodical precision, and after they had completed their job, another group of largely older people boarded the train in a great hurry. During that time a police officer came by our car and apologized for the inconvenience. He wished us a pleasant trip, said his religious "Heil," and moved on. Immediately thereafter the train moved out of the station.

I emptied the balance of my vodka and threw the empty bottle out the window. The Germans in our compartment, apparently made drowsy by the steady motion of the train and the vodka, went to sleep. Leon and I just sat there looking at each other and tried to give the impression that we were not interested in what was going on around us.

To avoid any unpleasant surprises, we decided not to proceed all the way to Warsaw by train. Instead we left the train in the suburb of Rembertow and

walked to Stan's house. It was then already March 1943, and the beginning
of a new segment in our lives.

When Leon and I arrived in Warsaw from Terespol, the Warsaw ghetto
population had already been reduced to about 40,000 mostly young people,
some of whom were children. The ghetto, or what was left of it, was hermetically sealed. Almost every meter of the wall on either side was watched; for
anyone to get in was completely out of the question. Every morning one could
see a column of Jewish men and women marching to some job under a heavy
guard consisting of either German and Polish police or Latvian or Ukrainian
SD troops. Those young people were considered the lucky ones, since they had
been allowed to live—but for how long only the Nazis knew. They had not yet
been destroyed because the German factories were using them for the Nazi war
effort. Of course they received no pay, and how they managed to stay alive under
such inhumane conditions will remain a mystery for eternity.

For reasons of security for both Stan's family and for ourselves, I decided that we were going to have to divide company. We agreed that I would stay
with Frank on Mlynarska Street while Leon remained with Stan. At dusk we
went with Stan by streetcar from Wawer to Wola, a trip encompassing the
entire city and its suburbs. It took almost two hours. Our arrival at Wola too
was a surprise visit, since neither Frank nor his neighbor had been notified
in advance of our coming. But I knew the attitude of those people, and I knew
that I was a welcome guest.

With no intention of remaining in Warsaw permanently or even for an
indefinite period, we were firm in our resolve to try to leave the overpopu-
lated jail and cemetery called the Generalgouvernement. Yes, "cemetery" was
the proper description for that which had once been a beautiful land. I do
not believe that Poland, in its long history, had ever before experienced anything similar to what it had been subjected in the last several years. We concluded that our further presence there was fraught with mortal danger and
that at any moment we could be dragged down into that dark abyss.

The Nazis not only coerced slave labor but also had organizations that
recruited the work force badly needed in Germany and elsewhere. They
formed firms with Polish-sounding names that advertised in the Polish press
to entice Poles to volunteer for work in different parts of Europe. One such
ad, offering jobs in France, caught my attention. I promptly answered it but
found to my chagrin that to get hired I would have to furnish two things: a
certificate from the Arbeitsamt, the Nazi labor office, and most important, a
clearance from the Gestapo office on A-Szucha Street. They were evidently
particular as to whom they let into France, and under the circumstances I
could produce neither document.

When I noticed an ad in the afternoon edition of the *Kurier Warszawski* that offered jobs in different parts of Europe for men of varied crafts and professions, I decided to look into it. The name of the firm was given as Jonas Ferret and Company, a business with headquarters supposedly in Hungary. They gave the Warsaw address as 1 Marszalkowska Street, in the heart of the city, with offices on the second floor.

At my arrival I found a line of people blocking the corridors and stairways waiting to get in, but the office personnel seemed to be quite efficient in processing the applicants. When I finally entered the office, I realized the reason for their efficiency. The young men and women in charge requested no identity cards or other documents and asked only a few routine questions.

They asked me whether I spoke German, and I confided to the young fellow behind the desk that I did. He then suggested making it a part of my application and told me that because of it I probably would be designated as the leader of a transport group. He also informed me that our final destination would be Skoplje, Yugoslavia, a place I had never heard of before. But first we would have to go to Berlin for processing. It made no difference to me now where I went, as long as I could get out of Warsaw.

After my registration was finished, I was handed a slip and asked to report back to the office two days later, when the group was to depart in a bus for the railroad station. I was told that there we would receive the required papers for further travel. I asked them whether I could get a friend of mine included, and they assured me it would be possible; I had only to give them his name and the same type of information they had gotten from me. I called Stan that same afternoon and asked him to come see me the next morning, since I did not want to risk taking a trip to Wawer on the eve of our departure. After I explained everything to him, Stan agreed to bring Leon to the office on the assigned day.

There were twenty men of different ages assembled that eventful morning. The young people who had taken our applications were there giving us last-minute information about the trip. A German appeared and asked for me by name after mustering us close together. He handed me some papers that I read and found to be traveling orders for going from Warsaw to Berlin-Grunewald. We were informed that a man in a brown uniform would be waiting for us at the Warsaw Station East and that we would receive further information from him. Then we all left together in a bus for the station in Praga.

The bus carried us quickly through the city east to our destination in Praga, where the brown-uniformed man was waiting for us. He asked the bus driver for the group's interpreter, and the driver pointed to me. Introducing himself as Mr. Buse, in charge of Operation East for Jonas Ferret and Company, he gave me additional instructions as well as food stamps, which we promptly redeemed. He added another group of thirty men who were recruited from a different town, and I was supposed to see to it that all the men reached our destination in safety. We took our places in a large Pullman-type railroad car, and shortly afterward we were rolling along to Berlin.

## PART 2

# Germany

# 9 Back to Berlin

I had spent most of my young life in Berlin and now was returning after a fourteen-year absence. In my youth it had been a wonderful city in which to live, and I recalled many pleasant memories of my days there. In time I had even managed to adopt the characteristic Berlin accent. There were plenty of beautiful cities in Germany, but none had that special something that made Berlin feel so alive. The people too were different from those in the rest of the country; the Berliners seemed to be a breed all to themselves, generally extroverted, exceedingly friendly, and very easygoing. The Berliners were also blessed with striking natural surroundings. There were a number of lakes, two rivers, and abundant forests that were kept in perfect condition to enhance the entire area and preserve the natural beauty. I used to board a boat on the Wannsee on weekends for a moonlight trip with music and dance. It was almost a carefree life in Berlin in those days.

Leon woke me from my dreams to tell me that the men were hungry. At the beginning of the trip I had put a young man from Krakow named Waclaw in charge of food distribution. This nineteen-year-old lad later turned out to be very handy indeed. Although he was bordering on juvenile delinquency, I believed that I could handle such a boy better than a sedate one, provided that I was willing to meet him halfway. I asked Waclaw to distribute the food and cigarettes, and then I interviewed each and every one of those fifty men, since I wanted to know them a little better. They were a fairly good cross-section of Polish working people, with the addition of a few peasants.

After a while I again turned my thoughts to Berlin. We had just left Landsberg Station on the Warthe River; that meant we now were very close.

The happy-go-lucky life in Berlin in the early and midtwenties slowly began to change after the election of the then field marshal General von Hindenburg to the presidency of the German Republic. The military aspect of life was reemphasized. Some of my friends joined paramilitary organizations, and their behavior suddenly changed; they assumed an air of secrecy. My roommate, Albert Hartmann, a young man from Zwickau, joined an outfit called the "Stahlhelmbund," which held regular military exercises every Saturday and Sunday.

In the midtwenties a never-ending prosperity seemed to reign in Germany, disturbed only through periodic bickering in the lower levels of the political spectrum. This was the beginning of the ascent of the Nazi Party. Albert Hartmann and I worked for the Siemens and Halske Company, a large concern in Siemenstadt, and the changing situation began to be reflected in the plant. At first the workers were organized by the then democratically controlled unions, but soon there appeared another union known as the "Yellows." The Yellows, organized by the Nazi Party, were used mainly for strikebreaking and had the full support and protection of the management. Once in a while the Yellows would bring down some of their bigwigs and organize a meeting at the plant, something the other unions were not allowed to do. It was the Yellows who broke the back of the famous 1926 strike at the Siemens and Halske plant.

The Nazis organized the infamous SA—the Sturmabteilungen, or storm troopers—to terrorize their enemy, the Jew, and any group that opposed violence. The Nazis were also set against the communists, who in turn organized their own uniformed troopers named the "Spartakusbund." For several years before Hitler came to power, these two groups fought violently with no end in sight. In addition the SA indirectly fought the Jews by desecrating Jewish cemeteries and synagogues in Berlin and other cities. Such destruction was usually explained as the work of pranksters.

There was no special sector for Jews in Berlin, but in Berlin-Mitte, the center of the city, the stores were owned mainly by Jews. Frequently Jews were attacked, but even in 1928 those cutthroat Nazis were rarely arrested. In that year it was not safe to walk the streets in Berlin because of the frequent street fights. When I worked for an outfit called Ludwig Labischin Company, I used to get off the streetcar in the suburb of Lichtenberg at the corner of Mainzer (the street on which I had an apartment) and Frankfurther Allee. One day I could not cross the street because of a fight between the police, the Nazis, and the Spartakus men. The fight was taking place in the aftermath of a communist funeral procession, complete with red banners, which was returning from the burial of a youth killed two days before in a brawl with the Nazis. The most interesting part of that day's fight was watching the police beat up their own assistant police commissioner, whom they mistook for a Jew. This constituted only a fraction of the turmoil going on in Berlin at the time.

The progressive increase in anti-Semitic incidents provoked by the Nazis—which I witnessed almost daily—caused me to leave Berlin late in 1929. At first I had corresponded with my friends in Berlin, but after 1933 I thought it the better part of wisdom not to compromise those people by exposing them to harassment by the Nazis.

Now, after an absence of almost fourteen years, I wondered what major changes had taken place in Berlin. The train came to a halt at Anhalter Station, and to get to Grunewald I had to leave the train and take the subway to my destination. It was evident from the looks on the men's faces that they were rather pleased with my performance so far. I did not tell them that I had lived in Berlin before and therefore was fairly familiar with the city.

The Grunewald I found was a far cry from the one I knew years ago. It was no longer a dark green, almost impenetrable forest. Close to the subway station the area was interspersed with camps full of barracks, one of which, Lager Eichkamp, was my destination. I entered and reported to the representative of Jonas Ferret and Company.

One characteristic of Berlin's past was the city's mixture of different nationalities and races. Berlin used to be literally a cosmopolitan metropolis. The situation I encountered in Lager Eichkamp was in many ways reminiscent of those bygone days, except that freedom was missing. Otherwise, there were people representing scores of different ethnic backgrounds, with perhaps the exception of Jews and Gypsies. But with the addition of Leon and myself, the Jews were there too, albeit incognito.

The processing in Eichkamp took about three days and included registration, picture taking, and a medical examination. The exam presented a major problem for Leon and me, since looking for circumcision was the most elementary means to recognize a Jewish male in Europe. Although thousands were checked there each day, I was still afraid of the examination and tried hard to find some way to bypass it. The situation looked quite hopeless. Luck seemed to follow me, however. It dawned on me that I might find a way out of the dilemma with the help of our young delinquent friend Waclaw. I approached Waclaw and told him that we would have to get along without Leon since I was sure that the company would not let him go on. I said that Leon would have to go back to Warsaw and waited for Waclaw to ask me why.

"Well," I told him, "it's because Leon has a lung infection, and they are bound to see it. You recall how thoroughly they examined you." He thereupon asked whether he could do something for Leon, and to that I replied, "There might be a possibility. Let me think about it, Waclaw."

As an interpreter, I was busy preparing the others for the medical examination and was constantly on the go, milling around between the barracks and the infirmary. I had arranged for Waclaw to be in the first batch, and there were several hundreds after him. Just before the end of the day I sent him through again, this time for Leon. Everything clicked just right, and I had him repeat the process the following day for me after telling him that I had a slight venereal infection that would cause me to be disqualified also. So far Leon and I were in the clear. As of that time we both were bona fide OT men and wore the brown uniform of the OT Service; "OT" stood for "Organisation Todt," which was the branch of the government in charge of all construction for the Reich.

After three days at Eichkamp, we were sent to another camp, this time in the suburb of Schlachtensee. There we were assigned to permanent barracks, and I was told that we were to remain there for an indefinite period. The following day I received a call from the company to report to their office on Friedrichstrasse, where I discovered that the real owners were two German businessmen from Berlin, not Hungarians, as had been implied. One of the gentlemen was a Mr. Meenzen, a former Fiat automobile dealer whom everyone called Papa Meenzen, and the other was a Mr. Wiesner. Judging from their accents, Meenzen was a Berliner, whereas his partner was from some provincial town. Both were Nazi party members, but they seemed to be good men despite the party emblems on their lapels. I had a feeling they wore the emblem for business reasons only.

They asked me some questions about my qualifications and were especially curious about how and where I had acquired knowledge of the German language. I improvised some plausible-sounding reason but did not know whether they believed me. They told me that my destination was not certain, but I would be notified when and where we were going to be shipped. They also promised to find a job for me there at the headquarters at some later date, since they were just getting organized.

Such companies had an interesting relationship with the Nazi regime. The government called them "contractors." The OT furnished the contractors with transportation, food, clothing, and shelter and paid them a nominal sum based on hourly wages for each man. The contractor undertook to furnish the labor through advertising, and through coercion when necessary. Rather than pay the men anything directly, they supposedly mailed the money to their families. I gave the address of my friend Stan, and he never received a penny from them.

When I finally finished my interview with Meenzen and Wiesner, I rode out to Lichtenberg to learn whether my former landlord, Frederick Lange, was still living there. I noticed only one major change on the way; in former years I had to take the streetcar from downtown to my former residence in Lichtenberg; this time I made the trip in a brand new subway.

Luckily the Langes were still alive and living there. We were happy to see each other after so many years, particularly the motherly Mrs. Lange. I used to call her "Mutti" (mother) because she acted like one with me. Her husband was by then already retired from his railway job. He was a serious person; even his jokes were usually serious.

We talked about the past, but when the conversation turned to the present, Lange became quiet. We had lost some mutual friends because of the Nazis. In an almost inaudible voice, he said he was sure Hitler would not win the war. "Viele Hunde sind des Hasen sicherer Tod," he said. Roughly translated, it means that many dogs on the chase are a sure death for a rabbit. The Langes of course were aware that I was a Jew, and I knew their attitude well; otherwise I would not have risked going to their home for a visit. They had a married daughter whose husband, a banker by profession, was already a member of the Deutsche Nationale Partei many years before the war. I expected him now to be a Nazi, or at least a sympathizer, but he was on the Russian front, and I was glad not to have to tempt him.

Leaving the Langes, I rode down to Lichterfelde, where I had held my last job in Berlin. The company name was still there in big letters, but I was sure that the Jewish owners were no more. Next door to the company was a chemical plant, which back in the midtwenties was controlled by the Reichwehr (German Army). The only shipping from that plant had been done at night, and in that area it was an open secret that they were producing poison gas for the military. That plant too was still in operation. I noticed some bombed-out structures here and there, but they evidently were cleared of debris as quickly as possible so as not to mar the German spirit. One thing they could not hide any more was the acute shortage of everything except watered-down beer and toothpaste, of which they had plenty. Food was in very short supply.

Two weeks later we boarded a long freight train bound for Johvi, Estonia. This time we were supposed to be accompanied by an officer of the OT Service, but he left me in charge of the group and went ahead in a passenger train. The officer, who told me he was going to meet us at Riga, Latvia, apparently had decided that we were not likely to escape. The trip proved uneventful.

It was now March 25, 1943. The OT officer met us in Riga, and from then on we traveled together because there were no more passenger trains. It took us six days to reach Johvi, a railroad stop with a small station but no other buildings, located somewhere between Tallinn, the capital of Estonia, and Leningrad.

Johvi was a heavily wooded area in northern Estonia with tall, beautiful silvery birch trees. Located deep in the woods, and reached by dirt roads that the Nazis had laid out with timber to overcome the swampy ground, was a large clearing comprising perhaps thousands of acres. In it a completely new town was being constructed. The prefabricated barracks were set on stilts formed by leaving tree stumps at a certain height after the trees were cut down. The reason for all the frantic activity was the presence of a substantial deposit of brown coal, out of which the Nazis extracted oil for their war machine. In addition to the great number of German technicians, there were tens of thousands of foreign workers. Some of these were slave laborers, but a number were also volunteers of sorts. There was also a camp for Russian prisoners of war, whom they treated worse than animals. The Russians had to pick the garbage heaps and eat the putrid waste to stay alive. We were forbidden to help them under penalty of death.

The local population was several miles away. The few people who lived there were seldom seen. The Nazis supposedly were their liberators from the rule of the Bolsheviks, and in the process of liberation they had managed to take the different properties from the Russians. Instead of restoring the properties to their rightful owners, however, the Nazis kept them for themselves.

My assignment there was to serve as interpreter for the different nationalities whose languages I knew. I had plenty of work to do, since there were approximately a thousand Polish workers there alone. I also noticed that Leon and I were not the only Jews there, but we kept our identities to ourselves. Leon was given a job in the office, while I was mostly on the go.

At the beginning, even though we were surrounded by deep, almost impassable swamps and did not know the local language, we still entertained the thought that perhaps we could escape and cross the front line, which was only about fifty miles away. But shortly after our arrival we gave up on that idea when three men of a work group put such a plan into action. Caught in the woods by some local hunters, they were turned over to the Nazis, who hanged them in front of the office building.

The man in charge of this international slave and semi–slave labor force was an individual whose main job-keeping qualities were being a faithful Nazi when he was sober (which was a rare occasion) and having the voice of a lion with the vocabulary of a prostitute. After discovering his first quality, I made it my job to see that he had an unbroken supply of alcohol. It was not an easy task to find alcohol, but a few miles from our camp there was a small village where I managed to develop a barter arrangement with the peasants, using sign language. I traded tools for their moonshine products and food. The food was of a rather poor quality, but for us it was tolerable. Had someone told me before the war that one day I would be eating raw white meat with oatmeal bread, I would have thought him out of his mind. But here I was getting salted pork from an Estonian farmer in exchange for tools, and eating it without as much as a second thought. It was with such supplies that I kept that synthetic Prussian happy. In fact, he was a thoroughly Germanized Pole from the Mazury, a part of Prussia that historically was Polish. I believe he had an inferiority complex because his name was Perembow and not Schmidt.

About six weeks after our arrival in Johvi, an officer of our company in Berlin came for an inspection. Since I assisted him for the duration of his stay with us, I decided to take advantage of the opportunity by asking him for a leave to go to Warsaw for a few days. My request was readily granted. He took me with him to Berlin, where he prepared my travel order to Warsaw. All that took only four days. My main purpose for going to Warsaw was, first, to see my friends and, second, to see whether I could help anyone get away from that horrible place. I was now in a position to help, at least for the time being. In those days, almost nowhere outside the Polish borders was the terror as acute and as vicious as in Poland itself. The Polish territory was second only to the occupied territories on the eastern front in Nazi-perpetrated barbarism. In Warsaw my only concern was not to be recognized by some Pole who had known me from before the war, particularly ones who did not know me well enough.

My arrival in Warsaw coincided with the last week of the armed revolt by the Jews who remained in the Warsaw ghetto. On May 12, 1943, I was in my friend Frank's apartment on Mlynarska Street, directly across from the ghetto. The rattling of different types of weapons coming from the ghetto was clearly audible as the Nazis attempted its complete destruction. That last handful of Jews knew their situation was hopeless, but there was no alternative left for them. They refused to submit voluntarily to the process of elimination that was requested and expected of them. In less than one year, the Nazis had managed to march to the gas chambers several million meek people and destroy them without as much as a protest. Those people had gone to their destruction terrorized and spiritless. Then, a few thousand desperadoes provided a rude awakening for the Nazis.

The Nazis used every means at their disposal to break the resistance of a comparatively few Jews, whose actions came as a complete surprise to the murderers. The Schupo, or German police, were insufficient to cope with them. In addition to fighting the Schupo, the Jews of the Warsaw ghetto battled the SD, SS, Ukrainians, Latvian SS, Polish police, and Wehrmacht forces. Tank units were employed as well as artillery. Yes, the Nazis even sent the special pride of Hermann Göring into the skies against the handful of by now completely emaciated Jews.

All that was not enough for the heroic Nazis. To avoid exposing themselves to a fight, on May 12, the day of my arrival, they set afire a large section of the ghetto bounded in part by Smocza, Gesia, and Nalewki Streets. Despite their cruelty and desperate, murderous attempt, however, the Nazis were unable to speed up the destruction of those few Jews who engaged in such an uneven fight for their lives.

The ferocious battle of the Nazi hordes against the practically defenseless remnants of the once overcrowded ghetto went on throughout the day without respite. Fires engulfed the entire ghetto toward evening, the sky over Warsaw becoming one great flame. As if that hell on earth weren't bad enough, the city began to be attacked from the air. The Nazis stopped their bombardment of the ghetto as the air-raid sirens sounded, but now the noise of their barrage was replaced by that of Russian bombs exploding in different parts of the city. On prior occasions I had seen Russian bombers over Sokolow use flares to light up the railroad tracks they were targeting. This time they needed no flares to illuminate their targets, which were made clearly visible by flames of the burning ghetto. I was quite sure that the pilots above had no idea who to thank for those fires. For four days I watched that desperate but unequal fight from the window in Frank's apartment on Mlynarska Street.

With the help of Stan and Frank, I secured two young Jewish boys, made proper documents for them, and took them with me to Johvi by way of Berlin. Back in Johvi I found everything as I had left it, except that another transport had arrived in my absence.

Shortly thereafter Wiesner paid us a visit. At the beginning of my employment, Wiesner and Meenzen had promised me that I could expect a job in the home-office area sometime later, and I thought this as good a time as any to remind him of that promise. I hoped I could leave that place and go back to Berlin. I remembered seeing flowers on Wiesner's desk back in Berlin, so I cut some fresh flowers for his desk there in Johvi, believing that a closer relationship with him might possibly be beneficial to our cause. My strategy paid off a little later when I asked that he take me back to Berlin and give me a job there. "I could work out of the office," I said, "and be some kind of courier." He readily agreed.

The day before his departure, Wiesner told me to get ready to return to Berlin with him the next day. He took care of the necessary papers. The following day I picked up my travel order from our office. Leon made out the papers for me, and my alcoholic boss signed them. Finally, after a few uneventful weeks in Estonia, I was again on the road, this time for Berlin.

I arrived back in Berlin in June 1943, but not before experiencing partisan activity in Lithuania. Just as we arrived in Shouwli, our train's locomotive ran into a bomb that had been planted on the track. The locomotive and the first two cars were heavily damaged. Over twenty men were killed, and many others wounded in the explosion. As luck had it, Weisner and I were in the next-to-last car. It took eighteen hours to repair the damage and replace the locomotive and tracks before we could resume our journey to Berlin.

# 10    Three Times to the Rescue

I moved back into Lager Eichkamp on my arrival in Berlin. Some minor changes had taken place since I had left, but readapting required no major effort. The following day I reported to the office on Friedrichstrasse. I thought it strange that Meenzen wanted a report on Johvi, since his partner, Wiesner, had just spent several days at the camp, and I had given Weisner a full report while he was there. Meenzen pulled out a bottle of cognac from under the desk, poured me a drink, and told me to report to the office every morning at 8:30.

With no other income, I obviously needed money on a regular basis. The next day, my first regular day at the office, I asked Meenzen for some funds for my maintenance, and he ordered the bookkeeper to pay me on account, since they were not set up to pay their foreign employees regularly.

At first I had only to report to the office every morning at 8:30 and sit at my desk until noon doing nothing. Then I was free the rest of the day. I decided to move into a hotel and found a room in a medium-class one on Invalidenstrasse, not far from the Stettiner railroad station. After a couple of weeks of my vacation job, I was given the responsibility of meeting the trains loaded with foreign labor and receiving the incoming workers. I had to see to it that they were processed promptly and taken care of properly, since they were strictly voluntary and mostly skilled workers, as was I. I also was supposed to be in charge of them until they departed for their destinations. I must have done my job well, because one day Meenzen called me into his office and informed me that he had just nominated me as his representative in charge of the Jonas Ferret and Company recruits in Schlachtensee and Eichkamp. Quite an interesting relationship developed between me and those greedy bureaucrats.

Being in constant contact with the foreign workers in Berlin, I discovered that a cigarette or a cigar sometimes worked like magic in opening a door in either camp, and thanks to my connections with different foreign workers, I had access to many of the good things the average German could not get. I told Meenzen that everything was going smoothly because I did not hesitate to spend some of my own money for the benefit of the company. Since Meenzen's profit started the minute a man boarded a train out of Berlin for his ultimate destination, Meenzen readily opened an extra expense account for me. I also convinced the company to assign Leon to me, claiming that he was my first cousin and that he could be helpful.

With an extra expense account at my disposal, I enlarged the scope of my activity, learning more about the Nazis in responsible positions and penetrating that curious entity, the Nazi war machine, which by then was already in an advanced state of decay. Once in a while I took inventory of my own situation. Perhaps I was drawing too much attention to myself through my wheeler-dealer activities. Perhaps my success over others might provoke them to alert the Gestapo to investigate me. The Nazis would not have had to go far to do that; there was a Gestapo unit one floor above our office on Friedrichstrasse. Meeting some of their agents on the stairway every day made me quite conscious of the danger lurking there each minute I remained in the building. Unbeknownst to anyone else, I was on constant guard, ready to jump like a wild animal at the least sign of uncertainty. I was always conscious of my precarious situation.

My activities were prosperous for the company, and the attitude of Meenzen, as well as Weisner, helped me to become more independent. They trusted me to the point that when I submitted my weekly request for expenses, they did not even look at the amount; they just signed the request, and the treasurer gave me the money without question. As Meenzen delegated more and more authority to me, I was given the company stamp and letterhead so that I could make decisions on the spot without having to refer to the office first. I was also given the right to travel when and where I found it necessary. I took advantage of this by making frequent trips to Warsaw. Once I even went to Krakow to bring a young Jewish boy to Berlin so as to save him from the claws of local hooligans.

My involvement with him began when Leon called me from Grunewald about what he described as an urgent matter that he preferred not to discuss on the phone. When I got there, Leon told me that a young Jewish boy had just arrived from Krakow with a group of Poles and appeared to be in trouble. Leon had found out about him from some of his tormentors. They detected a Jew among them and approached Leon, not suspecting him of being Jewish also. The hooligans were hoping that Leon, being a stranger to the boy, would not hesitate in passing the information to the Nazis. The boy was in a group with another company over which I had no jurisdiction, but I thought that somehow I might manage to help. In any event, I would try. I asked Leon to instruct the boy to meet me outside the camp.

At that time I had no group at all, but I knew of a group of men in Schlachtensee, being processed by a different company, who were waiting to be shipped to a job any day now. I did not know where they were going to be sent, but I knew that the group was composed of French, Belgian, and Dutch men. I thought it reasonable to assume that the young man would have a better chance with those strangers than with others, and two days later he was on his way to Latvia, or so I was told. About a week later, however, I received a message of distress from him from Krakow. I brought him back to Berlin, and on the way he told me what had happened to him.

"When I left Berlin with that group of westerners, I thought I was in seventh heaven. I had no problem conversing with most of them, since French was my preferred subject in high school. The other boys were very friendly with me, and I enjoyed their company. None of them knew where we were going, and they seemed not to care. I did not realize until we got there that we were in Lemberg, the city where I had been born and raised. Walking down the street one day, I noticed one of my former schoolmates walking in the opposite direction. He attempted to greet me but I thought it best to keep walking and pretend I was not who he thought me to be. In light of that unexpected development, I realized that my continuous presence in that city was fraught with extreme danger. I left Lemberg that very same day and went to Krakow, where I had friends I could spend some time with. They were the ones who sent you the message on my behalf."

He did not realize that Leon and I also were Jews, since we had done our utmost to conceal our identity from him. In his opinion, we were just a couple of good Gentiles.

Jonas Ferret and Company maintained a small transient camp not far from Berlin in Falkenberg, a small town in Pommern. Judging by its location and beautiful natural surroundings, it probably had been some kind of Boy Scout camp before the war. An administration building and several barracks stood in the vicinity of a natural lake. Meenzen told me that the company had leased the place from some institution to provide vacation facilities for his employees at some later date. Whatever the truth was, I used it as a transient camp to lodge surplus laborers. I took that young boy to the camp and left him there in the hope that everything would be okay. I did not expect anything when I returned a few days later, but as was usual in such cases, something expected me. I was approached by one of the men in a very mysterious way.

He began by saying that he thought he could trust me and explained that they had discovered a Jewish boy in their midst. So far, only a few men knew, but he believed that it would then be too late to save him if more found out. I listened attentively, trying to figure out the proper position to take. I asked him why he had come to me with the problem, why he was not afraid to divulge that secret to me. He said that after having observed me, he concluded that I was a liberal-minded Pole who might be willing to help a young Jewish boy.

Not wanting to talk with the boy inside the camp, I asked him to send the boy ahead of me toward the station. I told him to have the boy wait there until I arrived and not to approach me until I gave him a signal to do so. That was how I got the boy out of the camp and back to Berlin. In 1943 Berlin was a hiding place one could trust. The city and its immediate surroundings were the safest places in Europe for a Jew to live, provided he had some documents that did not show him to be a Jew, because a Jew could not be distinguished from the great number of Mediterranean people who were then present in the city. Once in Berlin, I placed the young man under Leon's protection in Schlachtensee.

I could tell after I rescued him from Krakow that the boy did not quite trust me, but now, after this latest incident, his disposition changed completely. He turned to me and told me a story about his family, a long-held secret.

"When the Nazis were killing the Jews in Lemberg, my mother and a friend of hers and I managed to flee to Krakow. My father and the husband of my mother's friend had been deported to Auschwitz. While in Krakow, which was being subjected at that time to intensive Nazi terror, we decided to do something to relieve our friends of the dangerously grave responsibility of hiding all of us at their home."

The extermination process to which he referred was taking place during the most acute labor shortage the Nazi war machine had ever experienced. As the Nazis engaged in a macabre enterprise born out of insanity, they were cutting off their noses to spite their faces.

The boy continued his story, telling me that his mother and her friend signed up for jobs in Germany, leaving him with their friends until she could find a job for him too. Instead of waiting for his mother to help him, however, he did the same thing that she had done—sign up with a German company— and so had ended up in Lager Eichkamp in Grunewald. He now knew his mother's whereabouts, but she did not know his. Since he was afraid to write or telephone her, there was no way for her to know how close they were to each other. She was living and working in Pasewalk, a town not far from Berlin.

After listening to his sad story, I thought I knew what he expected of me, although he did not spell it out in so many words. That weekend I took a train to Pasewalk and had no trouble locating his mother and her friend. They did not know me, but a picture of her son and a handwritten message from him changed her disposition. I spent a few hours there and left my address and phone number with her before I went back to Berlin. I promised her I would bring her together with her son, and I managed to accomplish this in my hotel the following weekend.

Apparently this young man had a lucky star guiding his path. To my surprise, I was ordered to take a trip to Finland to deliver some important plans and other papers to a company mining camp located in Lapland, far north of the Arctic Circle. Obviously the operations of our company were quite extensive. I believed that this was a God-given opportunity to find a place of peace for that young man of ours. I was sure he would be safe in such a far-away place among the Belgian, French, Dutch, and Spanish workers who I was told made up the Jonas Ferret and Company labor force in Finland.

I had Leon make out the necessary papers for him, and we departed for Finland. We traveled by train from Berlin to Riga in Latvia, where we took a narrow spur rail to the Estonian town of Revel, called "Tallinn" by the Russians. I had been to these places before, but my passenger had not, and he seemed to enjoy it well. From Revel we took a boat across the Bay of Finland and into Hango. After three days in Hango, we took a train to Rovaniemi, which was already inside the Arctic Circle. I was somewhat confused, since I was under the impression that we had been going around in circles before we finally got to Rovaniemi, which was the end of the railroad line. Only a highway went north from there, and we were on our own to get to our destination, which was past a place called Ivalo.

The following day I located a covered truck going to Ivalo and arranged for a ride with the driver, who told me that Ivalo was about halfway between Rovaniemi and the nickel mines, our final destination. I glanced at his map and expected Ivalo to be a fairly large town since its name appeared there in large red letters. When we stopped, I couldn't believe that the town was Ivalo: there was nothing but a few frame houses, one of which was a roadside inn. We had to stay there overnight because night travel was prohibited on account of partisan activity.

The night in that inn was quite an experience. We were given a spotless second-floor room that had clean twin beds equipped with feather bedding. There was no electricity, so we were given a candle. We soon went to bed. I was almost asleep when I suddenly felt something like a needle prick on my leg. I was ready to dismiss it because of weariness (thinking it was just my imagination) when the pinching came back in full force, this time not only on my leg but all over my body. Still in the dark, I began to hit at whatever it was. Then I squeezed something that released an odor like a gas bomb. Jumping up, I lit the candle and looked at my bed. Then I realized that my sleep was over for the night. What I saw were different-sized bedbugs, running around like crazy to get out of the light.

We awakened the owner and asked for more candles, but instead he invited us downstairs into the lobby to spend the night in front of the fireplace with him. It was then the end of September, and in that part of the world it was already very cold.

The next day we obtained a ride to our destination, a mine located near the Norwegian border. It was in rugged territory with almost no vegetation except for some low-growing shrubs and weeds. After being in that camp only two days, my young friend knew that he would like it there. That place in the faraway north inspired within him a feeling of safety.

# 11     Escape to Italy

On my return trip from Finland, I managed to obtain a plane ride to Riga, and from there I traveled by train to Berlin. I had quite a scare when the train was redirected through Rastenburg, a city in East Prussia where, as I knew, Hitler's wartime headquarters were located. As soon as we stopped, we were literally surrounded by SS men from Hitler's bodyguard, the so-called Liebstandard. They allowed no one to leave, but they did permit someone to enter the train, which then departed in a hurry. I had never been as scared in my life as I was during the ten or so minutes we stayed there. When we finally left, it was more than just a relief. We were later told that damaged rails were the reason for the detour; whatever the real reason, I was sure it was not to pick up Hitler and give him a ride to Berlin.

The train picked up speed, and in no time we pulled into Schneidemühl, an important rail hub in Pommern. These were the days when the Allies had begun subjecting Berlin to intense bombardment. That fact, of course, did not make me unhappy, but the resulting misery, evident on that platform, was a different matter. As I watched people milling about, mostly women and small children getting off a train from Berlin, I heard a child's sudden outcry, a sound of razor-blade sharpness that caused me to shudder. That child's cry for its mother awoke in me all those memories of the recent past. I could not help but think of the tragedies suffered by a large segment of humanity because of this cruelest of wars, a war in which countless children had been thrown into a cauldron of fire and gas to their inevitable destruction. Glancing up from my thoughts, I saw enemies all around me. Executioners looked on through tiny windows while little angels were being annihilated. And here I was, contemplating the misery of this German child crying for its mother. I found myself almost crying, but the sudden jerk of the train brought me back to my senses.

Only a few hours later I was again in Berlin, and Leon and I began plotting our future course of action. We were reasonably sure that sooner or later we would be in danger of being unmasked and would end up before a firing squad or worse. The longer we stayed in Berlin, the greater the probability of discovery. We decided that we should be prepared to leave at a moment's notice if the opportunity presented itself.

I tried to take advantage of my position with the company as much as I could. I thought it would be better for us if I had a pistol, so I asked Meenzen to secure one for me. I reasoned with him that since I was a courier, often carrying valuable papers, and since the roads were rather insecure, I should carry a pistol for my protection as well as that of the company. Meenzen listened with interest and issued a certificate to the ordinance department of the OT for a pistol. I carried out that order immediately and received a 7.65-mm automatic and fifty rounds of ammunition.

Because of the nightly air raids, I stayed with Leon in Schlachtensee more often than in my hotel room, which was too close to the railroad station for comfort. I had been at my hotel during one such raid and heard the bombs falling all around me; those bombs had set an entire block adjoining Invalidenstrasse on fire.

On November 23, 1943, I was spending the evening with Leon, prepared as usual for the small harassing air raids. An old-timer from World War I who was in charge of the Schlachtensee Lager was discussing with us the situation recently created in Italy; most of the Nazis were furious with that turn of events on their southern front. Oddly enough, the usual alarm sounded almost the moment the bombs started coming down (until that time there always had been an interval between the signal and the actual bombing). The alarm sounded exactly at 7:45 in the evening, and immediately thereafter the searchlights began crisscrossing the skies.

Having been in Warsaw during the air raids in 1939, I naturally had more experience with such a situation than most of those around me. The air raids in Berlin, however, were not an entirely unpleasant spectacle to us. Although we would have certainly preferred that the bombs had built-in noses that could smell out Nazis from among the countless non-Nazis, such was an idle dream. But it was a dream shared by many others. We were quite sure that the French, Belgians, Dutch, Greeks, Danes, Norwegians, Russians, Yugoslavians, Czechs, Poles, and lately even the Italians belonged to that category of dreamers.

That night was for us a spectacle almost like an open-air theater. We were awed by the great magnitude of this air raid, which made the massive raids over Warsaw in 1939 seem insignificant by comparison. Judging by the sounds of the motors, there must have been over a thousand planes in each wave. Once in a while we would see the searchlights catch a plane and hold it until it was found by the antiaircraft guns. Sometimes, but seldom, a plane managed to escape by plunging into a low dive.

Since I did not trust our shelters, we had dug trenches almost two feet wide and six feet deep and covered them with heavy boards. We reasoned that this type of shelter would protect us from everything except a direct hit. Then, of course, we would not even know it.

It was all over in less than forty minutes. The only danger remaining to us was the falling splinters of exploded artillery shells. We picked up some pieces from the ground the next day, and we knew that the sharp edges were enough to kill even a horse. We didn't want to think of what would have happened had one of those pieces hit any of us on the head.

No bombs had fallen in the camp itself, but the surrounding area received some hits. Berlin, however, was subjected to a major catastrophe. From Schlachtensee it looked as though the entire city were ablaze. Berlin apparently was not prepared for such an event. Buildings in entire sections of town were just left to burn since the city did not have sufficient equipment to fight the fires.

Although Leon and I wanted to see the city while the fire was still burning, there was no rush, for Berlin would keep burning for several days. The day after the bombing we headed toward town, but it took us quite a while to get there with all the confusion. I checked our office and found the only person there was the janitor, a Dutchman who was living on the premises. After that we went to check my hotel on Invalidenstrasse and found that the whole street had been burned down, with not one building left intact. The damage wasn't limited to Invalidenstrasse, for all the side streets were completely destroyed for as far as I was able to see. Strangely, the nearby railroad station, the Stettiner Bahnhof, was only slightly damaged. A lot of people had saved themselves by seeking shelter in the subway tunnels.

My hotel building was still burning, and the owner was nearby watching his property going up in smoke. He was a staunch Nazi for whom I felt no sorrow, and I wondered what a man like him had in his mind at that moment. I wondered whether he recalled the countless mass meetings in which he and others like him yelled "Sieg Heil!" I wondered in how many synagogue burnings he had participated, and how much he had enriched himself by helping to despoil the countless victims of the Nazis during their heyday. I could not have cared less that the burning shell contained nearly everything that I could call my own.

As we walked away from the downtown area toward the west, we saw the same picture everywhere. Mostly women and children were sitting in the middle of the streets with the few belongings they had managed to save, though these were sometimes partly burned, filthy, hardly usable. I had to fight with my emotions to keep from crying out loud as I watched the misery.

The streets were full of people who appeared to be only visiting this once proud city in its hour of desperation and agony. But the streets were full of others as well, crying, visibly desperate, and utterly dispirited Germans, mostly old men, women, and children, the majority of whom were not properly clothed to keep away the chill. Finally, there were those who observed with mixed emotions that hell on earth, the result of the incredible gullibility of an otherwise intelligent people, a people who, in a moment of blindness, allowed an insane maniac to take over the reins of the land and assume power over their destiny. The faces of these other observers reflected a sense of cautious hope that the spectacle they were watching would contribute to a speedier end to the cruelest of all wars.

Always in my mind were the tragic events of 1939 and, more so, of 1942 and 1943 in Poland. Now in Berlin, as I observed the filthy semblance of human beings in the middle of the street, I saw columns of half-starved Jews— men, women, and children—marching to their deaths, prompted on by semi-wild dogs. Yes, I saw all those things and more, and yet I could not bring myself to discriminate in sorrow. Somehow I did not believe it right to place the blame on those miserable people for the sins committed by the Nazis.

Watching them drag the partly burned corpses from the debris, hearing the cries and lamentations, I could not but recall seeing the lighted sky over Treblinka with my friend Stan, knowing that the light came from the open-hearth furnaces of burning humans. That light could be seen for miles away, as could the light over Berlin now. But there was a difference. In Berlin the flames resulted mainly from the burning of wooden structures; humans got caught in that flaming Moloch only accidentally. It is right to assume that those brave British and American pilots intended to burn inanimate matter only, unlike the systematic, efficient, brutally premeditated slaughter executed in Treblinka and other such places of Nazi cultural endeavor.

The Germans could not start clearing the debris, because most of the city was still burning. In some places, however, the destruction was caused not by firebombs but by the so-called blockbusters. One such place was the OT command headquarters in Westereutz. The Ferret company got the contract, and I was in charge of the clearing job. I was given one hundred men, for it was quite a job. While I was walking through the ruins to assess the scope of the damage and decide how to proceed, I kept looking around for any printed forms that might be useful to Leon and me. I managed to pick up some blank travel forms and identity cards, as well as some official stamps.

Since from that day on I had no hotel room, I stayed with Leon in Schlachtensee. The airplanes came every evening with such regularity that we could predict their arrival almost to the minute. Then one day in early December an air raid came in broad daylight. The bombers supposedly were American.

At first Göring had promised the German people that they would be safe from enemy bombings, since the enemy would not dare bomb the Reich. When the first night raid came, he said that any criminal could sneak in at night, but no one would dare bomb Germany in the daytime. Then came the daylight bombings, and according to Hermann Göring, they were meant to add insult to injury. It had to be, he said, the Americans on direct orders from that arch-Jew Franklin Roosevelt. We knew these events added up to one thing—Hitler's end was approaching at a progressively faster pace.

Since Leon and I had it in our minds to leave Berlin in the near future, I wanted to see my former landlords again before we left. When I reached Lichtenberg, the suburb where the Langes lived, I could find nothing but empty, burned-out shells of the formerly beautiful apartment buildings.

Berlin had a system of leasing out vacant land to its citizens on a first-come, first-served basis, and anyone who wanted to develop a garden, or *Laube*, could qualify. The Langes had such a garden, since both of them had come from farm families. They had built a small shed on the land, and the city furnished all the utilities. I knew the location of their *Laube*, which, although small, was sufficiently large to accommodate a medium-size family in an emergency, so I decided to see whether they had sought shelter there from the disaster. I was sure that I would find them there, provided they had survived the bombardment.

They were both at the *Laube* and in good health, but Frederick Lange was naturally bitter and disgusted. He said, "You know, our Kaiser Wilhelm brought us to the point where all we could afford was *Holzschuhe* [wooden shoes], but the way the situation is looking now, Hitler will bring us to the point where we won't have any shoes at all." After spending several hours with those friends, I left them happy, knowing that they survived that holocaust.

Daily the situation in Berlin became more confusing. People looked at each other with growing suspicion, and I thought that I detected a certain coolness toward me by some of the office personnel, particularly those in high positions. It is quite possible that this was just my imagination, but they appeared to be watching me in a suspicious way. I shared my impression with Leon, and after a long discussion we concluded that we could not take any chances where our lives were at stake. We decided to leave Berlin for good— while there still seemed time to do so.

We had the necessary prerequisites. After filling out the various blank documents in our possession, we could be on our way to any destination within the German jurisdiction. Up to a point, we were the masters of our own destiny. The only problem was where to go.

After an exhaustive debate, we finally narrowed our choice to two countries: Italy and Yugoslavia. Yugoslavia appealed to us because of the partisan activity there, as well as the ease with which we could have adapted ourselves linguistically. Italy was attractive because of the latest happenings in that country; they had just thrown out Mussolini in a revolution and were trying to cut their bands of friendship with Nazi Germany. In such an atmosphere, we reasoned, we could eventually reach the Allied forces with the help of the local population. We decided on Italy.

I knew from my activity in Berlin that a firm by the name of Lorentz and Company, with headquarters in Danzig, had recently sent some men to Italy in the general area of Genoa. The following day I went to my friends the bureaucrats in Grunewald and found out the exact location of the Lorentz company in Italy. The company field office was in the province of Savona. On December 15, 1943, I filled out the documents and the necessary travel orders. The destination: Lorentz and Company, Savona, Italy.

The next evening we went to the Anhalter Station to board a train for the first leg of our journey south, to Vienna, but encountered a short delay because of an air raid. We were not happy about the interruption, but there was nothing we could do except wait. The air raid was soon over, and we were on our way out of Germany for good. We traveled all night, encountering several air raids on the way. Each time the train only slowed down.

We arrived in Vienna during the day and had to remain there until the following night. The next day we went sightseeing in that exquisite city, which neither Leon nor I had ever visited before. We saw the attractions that visitors to the Austrian capital usually visit, among others the famous Prater, an oversized amusement park in a beautiful natural setting. It did not make the impression on us that it probably would have made had the circumstances of our visit been different. The rest of the day we just killed time waiting for the evening train for Milan. Frankly, we were fearful of something we could not explain. I visualized that they had somehow uncovered our scheme in Berlin and were waiting for us this moment at the railroad station. That was a silly thought, of course. How could they know where we were, or even that we had left Berlin? No, it was sheer nonsense to entertain such foolish ideas. Still, we walked toward the station with mixed emotions. The answers we found for ourselves were insufficient to calm or alleviate our apprehension. Once more we stopped and checked our documents to see whether we had made any grammatical errors. Everything seemed in order.

We had observed the station the night before and noticed that the check-point was being watched closely. Every single man, even officers, had been carefully checked, documents as well as luggage. We arranged to be there at the last minute, when the crowd was the thickest and everyone was in a hur-ry. As we approached the checkpoint and I produced my document, I was completely calm, almost numb. After checking my papers and apparently finding them in order, the Nazi handed them back to me and, with a stony face, turned to the fellow behind me. The same procedure took place with Leon, and we finally boarded the train for Italy.

The trip through Austria was uneventful, except that whenever we stopped at a station, there was always a waiting train loaded with Italian pris-oners of war. That was the first time Leon and I had ever seen any Italian mil-itary men. But prisoners of war almost always look alike, no matter who they are. Those usually nice-looking Italians looked miserable. We were not aware of how long the Nazis had kept those poor young men confined before ship-ping them to Germany.

As it slowly began to get darker outside, we settled down in our rather nice and comfortable compartment. We alternately took naps. Only two other men, both soldiers who were assigned to the Italian front, occupied the com-partment designed to accommodate eight persons. After awhile I fell asleep, and Leon later told me I was very restless. He said I must have had an un-usually bad dream, which was likely considering the constant pressure un-der which we had been living. Like everything else in this world, however, dreams also come to an end.

I awoke suddenly to Leon's announcement that we were in Italy. I opened the window and read in large letters "Tarvisio," the name of the station. At the same time I heard the periodic knock of a hammer and a man singing a song. The song he was singing had been familiar to me for many years—it was the very melodious "Santa Lucia." In my lifetime of travel I had seen many railroad inspectors inspecting the wheels of railroad cars. This being a routine job, one would not expect any special expression of happiness, es-pecially a song, particularly at one o'clock in the morning. But that actually happened at the Tarvisio station, and suddenly the persistent feeling of de-spair that had often accompanied me during the last few years began slowly to melt away. The realization that survival was a strong possibility changed my disposition. I expressed my feeling to Leon that a country whose people have songs in their hearts while performing simple work late at night must have people who are bound to be nothing but good.

Many years ago while living in Berlin, and still very young, I had been a member of a choir, or *Gesangverein*. We had a motto for new-member initiations that came back to me as I listened to the pleasant baritone voice of that obscure Italian worker at the railroad station in Tarvisio. It went:

*Wo man singt, da setze dich ruhig nieder*
*Denn böse Leute haben keine Lieder.*

Translated, it has approximately the following meaning:

*Wherever you hear people singing*
*Take your place without fear*
*Since it's only bad people*
*Who have no song in their hearts.*

# PART 3

# Italy

# 12 Arrested Once More

We arrived in Milan early in the morning of December 20, 1943, and reported to the Lorentz company agent. It was a routine matter, and we were promptly processed for further travel to our final destination—the city of Savona.

By afternoon we'd reached Genoa, but for administrative reasons we had to stop in Varazze and stay there overnight. At the main company office in Varazze, we were added to a roster and told to report to a man named Fichtner in Savona, where the engineering offices of the Lorentz company were located. That night we were given separate hotel rooms because of the entries we had made in our forged documents under the heading "Nationality." We had decided that I was to be a *Volksdeutscher* so that I could continue to carry my pistol legally. Leon, whose German was not quite as clear as mine, was to be a Lithuanian. We were given separate rooms because to a Nazi, assigning a German to a room with a non-German would be simply preposterous. That evening Leon and I indulged in the delicious Italian red wine to an extent that it may not be best to describe.

The next morning we were taken by car to Savona, where we were promptly introduced to Fichtner, a civil engineer who managed the office. He was visibly elated to see us, particularly since he had expected no help from any quarter. He assigned us rooms in the military compound on Corso-Rici, the location of both the company offices and OT headquarters. Also stationed in the same compound was a company of Bersaglieri, Italian troops who stuck

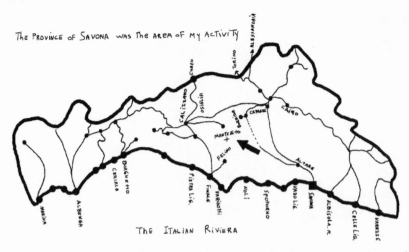

Map of the Province of Savona, Italy, drawn by the author. The arrow points to the approximate location of his partisan command headquarters.

with Mussolini and, by implication, with the Germans. The Bersaglieri were there in the compound to protect the Nazi forces. Corruption was widespread, both because they were badly underpaid and because they were watching their nation being torn asunder by the rudeness and cruelty of the Nazis. Everything those Bersaglieri had was for sale—no questions asked.

Fichtner was in the organizational phase of a project he was to complete for the German military authorities. He outlined to us his assignment: to build a system of fortifications extending from Savona to Varazze. Since the complete design of the entire project had already been delivered to him, there was little for Fichtner to improvise. He needed only to organize the work force, materials, and shop drawings. Leon was available to produce the shop drawings, and I was given responsibility for the outside organization. While we awaited the signal to start the project, I was assigned a group of workers and given the job of keeping the railroad tracks in working condition. Almost every night we repaired the damage that the American bombers had done to the tracks during the day.

For the time being, Leon and I did not worry about being detected. The Nazis were already beginning to lose control. Besides, a company that was paid by the government for each man on its payroll would not initiate an investigation to discover why two men from Berlin showed up on the job without request. The company officials probably assumed that they had friends in Berlin-Grunewald and thought it the better part of wisdom not to be too inquisitive.

Fichtner consented to my request that I move out of the military compound and locate myself in an *albergo*, or inn, in the town of Celle-Ligure,
which was the center of my activity. After a couple of weeks, I managed to
have Leon join me there. My next job was to prepare the preliminary groundwork for a defensive wall along the beach as well as defensive bunkers in the
hills facing the Mediterranean coast. In the meantime, they extended my
sector somewhat more south of Varazze. Still, the work thus far was preliminary, since the Lorentz company as yet had neither the materials nor the
workers necessary for the job.

With plenty of time on my hands, I plunged deep into a study of the Italian language and spent hours reading whatever was available. I also hired
some aides for my field office, although I had nothing for them to do as yet
other than help me learn the language. Learning Italian did not prove too
difficult because I still remembered some Latin from my school years. I soon
concluded that no other people in the world would go to such lengths to make
themselves understood as the Italians. They might speak Italian to you, but
the expression on their faces and the movements of their eyes and hands were
definitely geared to international understanding.

Slowly the expected workers began to arrive in a classic repetition of
events and systems used in Poland, involving even the same companies. In
this particular case, the Lorentz company was awarded the contract because
of the job's technical characteristics. But most of the people they brought
down to the coast were farmers from the area of the Piedmont, and they too
had their contractor, a Mr. Vigano. As time went on, Vigano would indicate
to me that he hated the Nazis and that he was not a Fascist. To me it mattered little whether he was a Fascist. What interested me was that he claimed
to hate the Nazis.

When all the workers were finally assembled, the order came to start work
immediately. The Nazis had to depend on older, foreign, and largely hostile
laborers to accomplish their goal of fortifying the coast. The only real German on the entire project was an old carpenter foreman who was under my
jurisdiction. The beach wall was to be about ten feet high, four feet of which
was to comprise the foundation below ground. The wall was designed specifically to prevent enemy tanks from reaching solid land after disembarking
from their landing craft. The wall was to be topped with sharp, broken glass
to prevent marines and infantry from jumping to safer points and establish-
ing a beachhead.

Once completed, the concrete bunkers in the hills would be an integral
part of that defense scheme. We were to build two kinds of bunkers, one
designed for heavy machine guns and the other for 75-mm cannons. They

were to be placed in such a way as to keep the coast under cross fire in case of an attempted landing by the enemy.

The work proceeded feverishly day and night while we played hide-and-seek games with the American fliers. They made a habit of coming over from Corsica at least seven times a day on their bombing runs to the Savona port area, which the Nazis used to supply troops in the south by way of motor barges traveling at night. Sometimes the Americans dropped a bomb on our job.

Not far from my field office was a marina operated by an older gentleman. I noticed that there was a small boat with an inboard motor in his shop. That boat triggered the idea that—with some knowledge of navigation and a little luck—we could easily take the boat to Corsica and be safe from the Nazis for good. I mentioned my thoughts to Leon, who did not seem to like the idea; nevertheless, once the idea had come to mind, I found it hard to brush aside. I had two fine young men working in my office. Both were local people and former navy men, so I decided to feel out their opinions regarding such an undertaking. My decision to confide in them brought me more than I had hoped for: they became my co-conspirators.

The immediate problem was obtaining the money needed to buy the boat. With the help of Vigano, however, we managed to sell enough of the material from the job to pay for the boat and other equipment needed for the voyage and still have some money left for an emergency. Vigano had been the only man it made sense to approach with such a problem, since by his own admission he too hated the Nazis. Of course, he could not be told the whole story. For some inexplicable reason, I had reservations about Vigano. Perhaps because he was a contractor for the Nazis, a nagging suspicion was continuously in my mind that, as a practical businessman, he should not be completely trusted. But I was put at ease when he was personally compromised by procuring money for the boat.

The next day Vigano handed me a stack of Italian lire. I had never seen that much money at one time, but it took a lot of lire to purchase just a little. I paid for the boat and thought that we were almost ready to go, despite Leon's continued reluctance to participate in the adventure. I had made up my mind, and nothing short of a disaster would have stopped me.

Bad weather delayed us for several days, and in the meantime a set of unusual circumstances began to develop. Almost every day a German officer appeared on the job, looked around, and asked me for certain people of whom I had never heard. I began to worry that perhaps the Nazis had found out that I had bought the motorboat and were shadowing me to discover my intentions. But I pushed aside such reservations and kept telling myself that I had nothing to fear. Leon continued to pressure me to desist from such a dangerous undertaking. Indeed, his objections were often quite logical. He even had one of our mutual friends try to get me to change my mind. Nevertheless, I continued with my preparations while sometimes resenting the negativity with which some of my friends approached my idea. I told Leon that if for some reason the journey should not materialize, then I was going into the mountains to join the partisans. I had already tried on several occasions to contact some of the partisan groups, which by now were active in the area, but had not met with success.

On one such occasion, I was ordered to repair a railroad bridge that had been damaged by the partisans. I proceeded with a group of fifty men in two trucks toward the bridge, which was located high in the mountains on the road between Savona and Ceva. Along the way I was hoping that we would be hijacked by partisans, but nothing happened. We arrived to discover that the bridge was not just damaged—it was totally destroyed. The partisans had done a thorough job, and we had neither the equipment nor the material to replace it. In addition, most of the men at my disposal were farmers and therefore not technically trained for such work.

On the way back, I engaged Vigano in a conversation about the partisan movement in an attempt to find out how much, if anything, he knew about it. He claimed to be in contact with some partisans in the area of Mondovi and Cuneo, and he said that if I so desired, he was ready to put me in contact with them at any time. I took that promise both with reservation and hope.

Because of increased partisan activity around Savona, at about that time the German authorities decided to issue rifles to anyone on their payroll who wanted one. Leon and I applied, and we each received a small Italian-made rifle that was quite handy. We kept them in our hotel room, but I always kept my official pistol with me in its holster on my belt. Whenever I retired for the night, I placed it on the chair next to my bed (if I had been asked why I did this, I probably would have been unable to explain it). I had second pistol, too, which I had purchased from the Bersaglieri, a small-caliber 6.35-mm pistol that I kept strapped just below and behind my right knee. I always kept the hidden one on me, loaded but well secured. In addition, I had purchased plenty of ammunition as well as a few hand grenades in anticipation of the projected trip.

We were ready for our hundred-mile trip across the water and awaited a moonless night. The weather was the major risk factor, but it was impossible to get a weather report because of the war. Based on their navy experience, both my companions claimed that we had nothing to fear, since that part of the Mediterranean was usually calm at that time of year. I accepted their judgment implicitly.

On the night of February 12, 1944, I took the maps, navigation compass, and other gear from their hiding place and left them on my nightstand. Our departure was arranged for the following evening at 11:00 P.M. We were to meet at the old man's marina at half past ten so that we would have time to check everything before proceeding. I took a couple of aspirins and went to bed. I fell asleep that night with ease, despite the excitement generated by the feverish preparations of the last few days. I must have been in a very deep sleep since I did not hear the sound of footsteps in the corridor outside my room early the next morning.

A sharp, loud knock on the door awoke me around 4:00 A.M. I put on my trousers and walked over to the door, barefooted. The feeling I had when I opened the door is hard to describe. There stood five men: a German officer, a sergeant, and three enlisted men with bayonets fixed to their rifles. The officer, a captain, pushed me ahead of him rather gently. He asked me my name and then for my OT service book. He ordered me to dress since, I was told, I would have to come with him. I attempted to assert that there was some mistake, but he cut me short, saying the decision was not his to make. While I was dressing, I saw him take my pistol from the chair and look over the equipment I had laid out on the nightstand for the voyage. Not a word was exchanged between us as he examined those items. Leon lay in bed motionless, just looking. They did not give him any instructions.

I asked permission to wash, which was granted. When I was almost finished dressing, I suddenly remembered that I was carrying some foreign currency with me, American dollars and British pound sterling; to have it found on me would have placed me in a very precarious situation. I had to get rid of that money before they took me to Savona, for they would undoubtedly empty my pockets of everything I possessed. I asked permission to go to the bathroom, which was located in the corridor. This was granted, but one of the enlisted men was ordered to follow me. He entered the bathroom with me. I sat down on the toilet and asked him to please at least turn around and give me a minimum of privacy, since I was very embarrassed. Unbelievably, he not only turned but stepped out, although he did leave the door open. That gave me sufficient time to throw the money down the drain.

We went downstairs and got into automobiles that were parked beside the hotel. Outside I saw four more soldiers with fixed bayonets, two at the building's side entrance and two at the main entrance. The captain and two of the enlisted men got into one of the cars with me, while the others apparently entered the car behind us. That second car followed us closely all the way to the office in Savona.

Sitting there—in the rear seat between two Nazis—I tried without success to think of who could have tipped them off. Then I suddenly realized that I had not thrown away all my money; I still had some coins in a small money pouch. With a Nazi on either side of me, getting rid of it posed an almost unsurmountable problem. But I was able to improvise a plan. I reached for my handkerchief to blow my nose, and pulled the money pouch out of my pocket along with the handkerchief. This took quite a while because I was tightly squeezed in between two oversized men. After I cleared my nose, I placed the handkerchief back in my pocket and simultaneously pushed the money pouch between the seat and the seat back. I had little time to spare since we were already approaching their office in Savona.

The most puzzling factor in the whole affair remained their elaborate caution in apprehending me. Of course, I did not know what they had been told about me, but it must have been interesting, since the procedures they followed that morning suggested that they thought they were about to bag an international spy of great importance, not a poor substitute in the form of a Jewish refugee who was just trying to save his own life. Under different circumstances it is possible that I would have been proud of such distinction. At the moment, however, I was fully aware of my precarious situation. I was preoccupied with only one factor now—how to free myself before time ran out. And the chances for that looked slim.

The automobile stopped in front of the local office of the military police, which was located in a hotel diagonally across from a monument dedicated to heroes of World War I. The Nazis fully occupied one-half of the hotel's first floor. Once inside, I was placed in a very small, drab, dreary, and seemingly makeshift room—or perhaps my depressed disposition simply made it appear that way. In any event, a partition had been positioned to exclude daylight. Two hours passed before an officer came in carrying a pad. He introduced himself as an officer of the Geheime Feldpolizei (Secret Field Police), which I understood to be the military counterpart of the Gestapo. He was quite polite and correct. He asked some routine questions and I answered accordingly. To my surprise, he repeated the same questions several times, although it was obvious that I had nothing to add to my answers. After a while he left, only to return shortly thereafter with a new set of questions. I believe I answered these to his satisfaction, because this time he left for good.

Later that same morning, around nine o'clock, another officer appeared and told me that I was under temporary arrest and that he was going to take me to the local fort for investigative detention. He expressed the belief that I would not commit the folly of trying to escape, and he further demonstrated his belief in my common sense by not handcuffing me. I assured him that I definitely had no such design and told him I was sure that this mistake would be cleared up promptly so that I could go back to work as soon as possible. He seemed pleased with my attitude.

Outside, the same car that had brought me there was waiting to take me to the detention center, which, I was quick to learn, was actually a common jail. I apparently was considered an old acquaintance by the driver, who greeted me with a cigarette on my return to his car. They took me to the military compound on Corso-Rici. As many times as I had been there, I did not remember seeing a jail before now. It was a building with its own gate, just outside the compound on the left, which was guarded by two tough-looking Bersaglieri.

We parked in front and entered the second-floor office of the jail's commandant. The man in charge was a middle-aged sergeant sitting half-asleep behind a big desk. As we entered, he jumped up, saluting in a real Prussian manner. The officer handed me over to the sergeant and left wishing me well.

I was happily surprised to see the sergeant, since I had seen him many times before while I was staying at the compound next door. We had even had a beer or two together at the canteen. The sergeant and I talked for a few minutes, after which he asked me to empty all my pockets. He apologized for the request, saying that it was a rule he had to follow. I promptly emptied my pockets, and to make it more convincing, I turned them inside out to show him that they were empty. I placed the contents of my pockets on his desk while continuously engaging him in conversation. At one point I picked up my wallet from his desk, removed the money from it, and handed the money to him. There were two pictures in my wallet that I carried with me throughout the war. One was a picture of my son, and the other was of the little girl in the Warsaw ghetto to whom I had smuggled food until her death. I asked the sergeant to let me take those two pictures into the cell with me. I told him that they were both my children, who now were with their mother back home in Berlin, while their father was in a jail in distant Italy, not knowing why he was being held. He looked at the pictures, then at me, and with an evident expression of pity said, "Natürlich können Sie diese Photografien mit Ihnen nehmen" (Of course you can take them with you). Following that, he accompanied me to my cell on the first floor, which already had two tenants. After the sergeant closed the door behind me, I greeted them in as friendly a manner as possible, but their reactions were rather negative. They seemed to express a suspicious curiosity, and I left it at that to give them an opportunity to get used to my presence.

The jail mostly housed deserters from the Italian front, although some were there for committing minor crimes. Both my cellmates, I soon learned, were deserters. The older of the two was a sergeant from Halle in Germany proper. I could tell that he was intelligent as well as educated by the scrutiny to which he later subjected me, all the while retaining an amicable air. The other was a much younger man from the formerly Polish city of Bydgoszcz, which the Germans named "Bromberg." Short and stocky, like a real farmer's son (which he was), he was one of the lukewarm Germans who could always be found in the part of western Poland from which he had come.

I spent the couple of hours until lunchtime trying to find out exactly where I was in relation to the street. The windows were barred from the outside with metal blinds, making it impossible to see the street from inside the cell. I knew the courtyard would give me a better vantage point, but I did not know what privileges, if any, the prisoners had in the jail. I decided to try out the guard, and I knocked on the door to get his attention. I told the young Bersagliere who responded that I wanted to go to the latrine. He opened the door, locked it behind me, and led me to the latrine, remaining outside while I was there. This excursion enabled me to orient myself to the street, latrine, and jail building. The latrine was located about eight feet from the building. As I entered and again as I left the latrine, I noticed a tall masonry wall right next to it. I figured that on the other side of the wall there had to be a street—and freedom. The door of the latrine hung on the left side of the opening, and the door opened toward the wall. At that time a plan of escape began to germinate in my mind.

As I returned to the cell, I thought it best not to delay any further and immediately started a dialogue with my cellmates. The plan I had just conceived would require their full cooperation, since I could not carry it out alone.

My companions were worried about their own fate, and for good reason. They could expect one of only two results from their trials—they could either be sentenced to death or, if they were lucky, be sent to the eastern front and placed in a special detachment composed of prisoners from state penitentiaries (in 1944, the second alternative was tantamount to suicide). I did not attempt to ease their minds. I suggested that their best alternative was to get out of that stink hole, but they did not believe there was any chance to do so. I then outlined my plan without yet divulging the fact that I had a pistol.

Lunchtime interrupted our conspiratorial conversation. The food in the jail was not bad; it was similar to the regular German army rations, and slightly better than what they fed the Italians. After lunch we were let out into the yard for a half-hour walk, but not all the inmates were let out at the same time. Had they been, I would have known that Leon too had been arrested and was being kept in a cell on the second floor of the same building.

I asked my cellmates to look toward the latrine each time they passed it during their walks around the yard and to remember every detail. Before going back to the cell, we were given a few minutes to use the latrine again. That half-hour walk helped me finalize my plan in every detail. I could now see myself on the other side of that wall.

Back in the cell we immediately started to coordinate our plan of escape from the jail yard and then discussed how we would get out of the cell. My plan was finally approved unanimously. We would need to wait until after there was a change of guard later that evening. Although we did not know the exact time the guards changed, we did know that after the change there would be only one man to a floor. Together we worked out every detail, which I already had prepared fully. It just seemed more democratic that way.

While waiting I told my friends that I had a pistol strapped behind my knee, and that fact left no doubt that our undertaking would succeed. The guard changed at eight o'clock that evening, and while both guard shifts were present, they opened all the downstairs cells to let the prisoners go to the latrine. Instead of going outside, I laid down on the cot and acted as if I were sick. One of the guards came into the cell to ask why I did not follow the rest of the men and even offered some help when I told him that I felt sick. I declined his help and continued to moan. My companions came back into the cell around 8:15, and we were locked up again. From that time on we were constantly on edge.

The time went on slowly. We heard the clock on a city church ring the half-hour, signifying that only fifteen minutes had passed since the change of the guard. Things in the prison began to quiet down. The clock struck again, three rings this time, and then all was quiet. One could almost hear a mouse crossing the corridor outside. Once in a while I heard someone coughing. We would make our move when the clock struck nine. That was final.

At the sound of the clock, I laid down on the cot while the younger prisoner knocked on the door and called for the guard. The other fellow stayed by me and held my forehead. The guard soon came to the door and asked the younger man what we wanted. He answered by pointing excitedly in my direction, where I lay moaning and apparently in terrible pain. After he opened the door, the guard followed the young man to my cot and asked what was hurting me. I quickly pulled the pistol on him while the two other prisoners simultaneously grabbed and gagged him. I then knocked him out, but I did not strike hard enough to kill him. After all, he should not have been the one to pay for his masters' orders. We then tied him up, put him on the cot, and covered him with blankets before leaving the cell and locking it behind us. I threw the keys to the cell into the latrine, and one by one we climbed up the wall, using the latrine door as a stairway. Once on top, we jumped down onto the sidewalk ten feet below.

Our immediate goal was to reach my hotel in Celle-Ligure to get civilian clothing. All three of us were in uniform (I had on my OT uniform), but we were lacking our belts, which remained in the jail. There were side roads we could take to get out of the downtown area, but the only way we could get to Celle-Ligure was to take the one road that ran along the coast between the sea and the mountains. This was an especially risky undertaking since any military man, whether Nazi or Fascist, seeing three men in military uniforms without belts would have known that we were prison escapees. Also, when the young Bersagliere in our cell came to, he might manage to untie himself and sound the alarm before we could reach the mountains. Although we obviously preferred not to be confronted with such situations, we were prepared by virtue of being armed. We had two pistols and did not intend to give up without a fight if cornered.

Fortunately we reached the hotel without incident. Everything seemed to be peaceful and quiet when we arrived in Celle-Ligure, but we approached my hotel very cautiously. I thought it would not be safe to enter the hotel, so I knocked at the window of the manager and asked her to bring down my civilian clothing. She did as I requested and told me of Leon's absence. With bundles under our arms, we took off toward the mountains and freedom.

Even though the mountains began only a few blocks from my hotel, there was one more obstacle to overcome: between us and the mountains was a Carabinieri post. Not knowing the service schedule of those state police was a handicap, but we managed to pass by undetected. We crossed past their post separately, leaving a few minutes between one another. I was the last one to move across, and we went into the mountains together.

In a short time we reached a height where it was safe to stop, catch our breath, and change our clothes. We threw our uniforms into a gully without even caring whether they were found the next day. We suddenly felt free. There was something about the mountains that inspired men like us to feel the way we did, particularly after an experience under the Nazi regime, with all its horror and tragedy.

After I once again started to feel that I was the master of my own destiny, I began to think about Leon. Although I tried to console myself with the hope that perhaps he was spending the night with some mutual friends of ours in Savona, a nagging suspicion led me to assume that he too had been arrested. I made up my mind to find out about him as soon as I could.

We rested for a while and then took off for higher ground, walking in the dark for several hours until we found a safe place to sleep. This turned out to be a haystack. We burrowed in and slept until morning.

As we pushed our way out of that haystack, we discovered to our great surprise that we were only a few feet from a village. We circled around it and proceeded on a northwesterly course toward the Alps. Our first stop was at an old secluded farmhouse. The only person there was an elderly lady who stood waiting in the door, watching our approach. She was obviously fearful, and we did not attempt to enter her home. After we explained that we wanted to buy some food and something to drink, she handed us some bread and cheese as well as a bottle of red wine. I asked her how much we owed her, but she refused to take any money. After thanking her, we proceeded until, a short distance from her house, we encountered a Carabiniere in full regalia. Carabinieri really are a colorful sight when fully dressed. We stopped a safe distance and observed him carefully. He smiled at us and indicated that he had no ill feelings toward us. He also told us he knew who we were and that he had been sent out on patrol that morning to try to arrest us. But he said that he was no friend of the Nazis or the Fascists and did not intend to harm us. Despite his friendly attitude, we kept our fingers on our triggers to avoid any surprises. After we got through complimenting each other, we took his pistol and rifle and bid him good-bye.

One major hurdle remained on the road to complete freedom. We had to cross the busy highway running from Savona to Alessandria and on to Turin. This we managed without incident. We had a carefree journey the rest of the day. We walked all day without stopping, until we came on an old shack in the woods. Everything seemed to be clear in the immediate area, so we laid down to rest on a bed of chestnut leaves that filled the shack. My thoughts again turned to Leon.

The next day, hampered by torrential rains, we walked on, wanting to reach the highest possible ground in the shortest possible time. I knew the mountains there were five to six thousand feet high, and we made that our immediate goal. Finally, late in the afternoon, tired and wet, we stopped at a farmhouse on a plateau. We were graciously received by the people there. The farmer's wife invited us into the house and offered us clothing to wear so that we could dry our own. She also fixed for us a big pot of polenta. While we ate, we were told that they had already heard of our escape from the Corso-Rici jail. According to their version, the Nazis had arrested a British spy, whom some of the local people had known to be a captain of the Polish Army, in Celle-Ligure, but he had gotten away that very same day. They also had heard that he had freed two other spies by putting the jailer in their place, and all three had escaped into the mountains. This was the reason for the unusually friendly reception we had received. It demonstrated to us that the people were on our side.

I regained my bearings from the farmer. I was about five miles from the little resort town of Nola, which itself was seven or so miles from Savona. In

Nola there lived a young man whom I had employed as secretary in the field office in Celle-Ligure. I knew I could trust him, and I was sure that he could tell me what, if anything, had happened to Leon.

As I left my fellow travelers near the farm, I asked them to wait for me until the following day. I told them that if I had not returned by then, they should go on without me and I would find them sometime later. I walked down the mountains toward Nola, making good time, and reached Nola in just a couple of hours. I went straight to the boy's home on the beach.

His mother opened the door, and I asked to see her son. She hesitated, undoubtedly because my appearance was not up to par, but the young man had heard my voice and came running to the door. Visibly scared, he was unable to speak for a moment; he just stood there and shivered. Only after I assured him that this was to be a brief visit did he calm down. The main purpose for my visit, of course, was to find out about Leon. Otherwise, the trip would not have been worth the risk. He told me that Leon was in the hands of the Gestapo and that he was being held in the Corso-Rici jail in Savona.

That ended my search for my friend Leon.

After leaving that villa, I decided to go by train to Mondovi instead of taking the same road back up the mountains. Vigano, the contractor, had one of his residences in Mondovi, and I intended to remind him of his promise to introduce me to the partisans whom he claimed to know. To get to Mondovi from Nola by rail, I had to change trains in Savona, taking the one going to Turin via Mondovi. Changing trains in Savona would be quite a dangerous operation: Nazis were always present at the station and always outside on the platform snooping around when trains arrived.

It was Saturday afternoon when my train arrived in Savona. It stopped at the station opposite another train that had just arrived from Genoa on its way to Turin. That train, like those in Poland and other occupied countries, consisted of some passenger cars, usually reserved for Germans, and some cattle cars for the citizens. When it appeared that the train was almost ready to pull out of the station and the platform was clear, I quickly jumped across the narrow platform and into a cattle car full of people. What an incredible coincidence it was that the men in the car were all former workers of mine from Celle-Ligure who were on their way home for the weekend. Immediately they surrounded me and hid me from view to protect me from danger.

My appearance at Vigano's door that evening appeared to be not too happy an event for him. Once he regained his composure, he quickly ushered me into the house and drew the drapes after locking the door. He kept my true identity from his wife to avoid scaring her and introduced me as an acquaintance from Savona. When I was alone with him in his den, I asked him about the partisans, and he still insisted he was in contact with them. But as he talked I watched his sudden change of expression, and I knew that my trip to Mondovi and its associated risk had been for naught. I felt completely deflated.

Mrs. Vigano had prepared a fine dinner, so we ate and I tried to forget my miserable situation. He agreed to let me stay in his home, since there would be no train until Monday morning. After a tasty dinner washed down with good Piedmont wine, our moods changed to the extent that the fear he and I shared melted away. I was given a clean room with a comfortable bed and rested there two nights in a row.

Seldom during that disgraceful war did I manage to get by without problems. In almost all my adventures I had one incident or another. My return trip to Savona was to prove no exception. Halfway between Mondovi and Ceva, high up in the mountains of Liguria, the train made a routine stop at a small station. Two Bersaglieri entered our car, which this time was a third-class passenger car of pre–World War I vintage—in other words, a museum piece. The car was packed with men going back to their jobs, and as it happened, many of them had protected me on the trip to Mondovi just two days before. The two soldiers asked everyone in the car to ready their identity cards for inspection. With that pronouncement, my friends began to mill around in the car, and I joined them in that maneuver. The soldiers became so confused that they did not notice me changing from the seats of those awaiting inspection to those who had already been checked. Despite the relative smoothness of the operation, it seemed an eternity before the soldiers finally closed the door behind them and the train began to move again. Those Italian farmers, some of them still boys, performed a masterpiece of cloak-and-dagger work on my behalf. They were obviously aware of the importance of their accomplishment, as was evident by their expressions after it was all over.

The train next stopped in Ceva, a small hamlet high in the mountains. As I left the train, it was a great relief finally to walk away from so-called civilization a free man. I walked aimlessly in the general direction of the sea, where at certain points I could see the extensive waters of the beautiful Mediterranean sparkling in the Italian sun, the surface of the water calm and enchanting. As strange as it may seem, walking alone in that majestic wilderness without a care, I felt as if I had found a paradise. The area was full of various flowers, the chestnut trees were pregnant with buds announcing the approach of spring, and the ground around the hazelnut bushes was loaded with nuts just waiting for me to bend down and pick them up. The location was simply ideal: fresh air, freedom, and an abundance of food offered by Mother Nature.

Scattered in those mountains were various small farms. Actually, the term *farm* would be a misnomer, for the so-called farmers worked land belonging to others. They owned only enough to supply a small fraction of their necessities, usually one cow or a goat and chickens maintained by the lady of the household for their own use. For the balance of necessities, they worked for an absentee landlord, harvesting the chestnuts and delivering them to the city in a marketable condition. After the harvest they would produce charcoal and muriatic acid. Despite all they did, however, they remained poor by any standard, including the Italian. Sometimes I wondered whether those people were so good because they were hardworking and poor. Most of the time they wore a ready smile and a song graced their lips.

I was walking at a leisurely pace on a large ridge when I came to a small clearing at the end of which I noticed a typical Italian house hugging a higher ridge. I approached it almost unnoticed until a dog unleashed a barking barrage that could have, and probably did, disturb all the dogs for several kilometers down the valley. The dog's dutiful performance brought the entire family out of the house. I had never been afraid of a dog, so I continued toward the cluster of people.

As I got closer, they called the dog and sent him into the house. We exchanged greetings, and they invited me to join them at the dinner table. It did not surprise me when they told me that they knew who I was since I fit the description they had gotten of me through the grapevine. I had long ago accepted the idea that nothing in this world is impossible. They were an average-sized farmer's family, consisting of a father, mother, three girls (one of whom was married), and two boys. The younger boy was at home, while the other was in a prisoner-of-war camp because he had not joined Mussolini after the dictator was restored to power. The younger boy had been in the service too but had escaped before the Nazis could get a hold of him. Despite the remoteness of their place, and thus the relative security I could enjoy there, I decided to decline their offer to let me stay to avoid jeopardizing their safety.

There were many caves in that area, and their son helped me to find one under a rock ledge that was almost inaccessible. This I turned into my permanent base.

On one of my periodic exploration trips, I ran into my former prison inmates. I took them back with me to my base camp, and our number again was three.

# 13 Recruited by the Partisans

A few weeks later I was approached near the farm by two armed men who introduced themselves as members of the Comitato di Liberazione Nazionale (Committee of National Liberation). It was the first time I had ever heard that name, but I understood its meaning. They wanted me to follow them to a certain place to meet a representative of the CLN, so I went with them to meet that mysterious person.

After a short march we entered a house where I met a rather distinguished older gentleman. He introduced himself as Simon and his companion as Leone. Those were the only names they gave me. They claimed to be well-informed about me and wanted to know whether I would be interested in assuming command of a group of partisans who were already organized and active. Simon said they were all local men and almost all were formerly in the military, including a few who were former officers.

After an exhaustive discussion with them, I understood that I was supposed to be something of a dark-horse candidate in a political stalemate, a catalyst to bind loose ends into a harmonious entity. The only thing wrong with their proposition was that I was not Italian, and for this reason I had some reservation. I was frank with them and said that I did not believe myself capable of the job. Their attitude, however, left me no choice but to accept the position.

Simon took me by surprise when he suddenly began speaking to me in Russian, telling me that he knew I spoke the language. I was flabbergasted but lacked the temerity to ask him how he had found out. Much later I learned that Simon's real name was Carlo Farini and that he was the chief of staff of the Seconda Zona di Ligure (Second Ligurian Zone) of the CLN's army, known as the Corpo Volontario della Libertà (Voluntary Liberation Corps). Leone's real name was Gin Bevilacqua, but all the partisans operated under assumed names. I was to become known as "Enrico."

Simon remained in the house while Leone and I left for the partisan group a few miles away. While we walked, Leone informed me in some detail about the existing situation in his unit, which we reached after a march of an hour or so. The Distaccamento Calcagno was approximately equivalent in size to a regular military platoon and had been named in honor of Francesco Calcagno, an anti-Fascist citizen who had been shot to death in reprisal for partisan activity in Savona. Leone assembled the men so that I would have the opportunity to meet them all together.

During the process of assembly, I noticed a disregard for discipline, which is so necessary in any organized group, and even more so in a group of partisans. Because of their relaxed attitude, they were unable to coordinate their activities and therefore exposed themselves to otherwise avoidable punishment by the enemy, despite their superior knowledge of the terrain. It was obvious to me that they needed an outsider to create a unified, responsive group, and that was the reason they had asked me to join. The reception they accorded me was encouraging, and I decided not to resist their "military draft." For a command post I was given a tent with all the usual things appertaining to such a position.

The next day I assembled all the 117 men in the detachment and gave them a speech, as best I could with my half-broken Italian. I was not exactly an orator, but my speech—delivered in a sharp foreign accent to a captive audience of men mostly younger than myself—held their undivided attention. I outlined my ideas for the organization as best I could, informing them, in essence, that force was the only thing the enemy would respect, that the only way to be forceful was through unity of purpose, and that the only road to unity was discipline. Henceforth, I said, the group would be divided into a number of smaller units, each with its own leader who would be responsible to a central command. The command, which I separated from the rest of the men, was composed of the commander, a second in command, a secretary, one man for logistics, and one for intelligence. In addition, I included a *staffetta*, or courier. I explained that, because of the nature of our existence, the rules and regulations that I might issue periodically would have to be obeyed, since this was the only way of successfully beating the enemy and achieving final victory. Furthermore, I told them that if they should decide at any time that I was not the man most capable of leading them, they should not hesitate to let me know. I would then step down, content to remain in their midst as a soldier in the fight against the common enemy. I then dismissed them, and they responded to my speech with a roaring ovation. I have to admit that I was quite pleased with their reaction.

I spent several days studying the situation, especially the locations of the different enemy encampments. I also spent a great deal of time getting acquainted with the men. Soon thereafter, having made the necessary arrangements for my absence, I left for a missionary tour to visit several bands that were scattered over a triangular area between Savona, Millessimo, and Albenga—an area I considered to be the elbowroom we needed both for safety and maneuverability. It was quite a large area containing several different politically controlled groups, which in the long run I thought could be harmful to the cause. I succeeded in bringing five different groups together for a conference from which a coordinating committee for action was formed. That enabled us to strike at the enemy with a force he never before had experienced.

Our increased activity attracted more and more young men, some of whom came to us out of a genuine desire to fight the enemy and some of whom came seeking action and adventure. Still others came to escape deportation to slave labor camps in Germany. Whatever their reason, we took them all and incorporated them into our ranks after proper screening and indoctrination.

By May 1944 we had reorganized our approximately three hundred men into a brigade consisting of four separate detachments. I thus became commander of the 20ª Brigata d'Assalto Garibaldi (Twentieth Garibaldi Assault Brigade). In August the brigade changed its name to the 2ª Brigata d'Assalto Garibaldi. Our numbers continued to increase, so much so that by late summer 1944 processing the men in the swelling influx became a major problem. To alleviate the congestion, I ordered that a secondary camp be established for new arrivals and made sure that we staffed that transient camp with some of our more intelligent men. After a period of investigation, those who were accepted were assigned to one of our detachments.

At the end of the summer, we reorganized our brigade of then over seven hundred men into four Garibaldi Brigades: Libero Briganti (third), Daniele Manin (fourth), Baltera (fifth), and Nino Bixio (sixth). I assumed command of the fourth brigade, which included the original Calcagno detachment, as well as three others (Rebagliati, Maccari, and Guazzotti), for a combined force of approximately four hundred men. I appointed as my second in command Radomir Saranovic, a former lieutenant in the Yugoslav army who came to us after escaping a prisoner-of-war camp. At that time we were under the overall command of a Colonel Zinnari of the Second Ligurian Zone in Genoa.

Comandante "Enrico" (author, holding Sten gun) of the Gin Bevilacqua Garibaldi Assault Division, near Tagliate, Italy, outside his mountain cave command post between March and April 1945. He is flanked by successive political commissioners "Renna" (Armando Botta, left) and "Vela" (Pierino Molinari, right).

"Enrico" (center) with his arms on the shoulders of vice commander "Radomir" (Radomir Saranovic, right) and vice commissioner "Candido" (Giovanni Urbani, left).

"Enrico" (far left) with logistics officer "Mirto" (Giovanni Carai, far right).

"Il Tigre" (Rosolino Genesio).

Brothers "Jim"
(Pasquale Figuccio,
right) and "Stiv"
(Stefano Figuccio,
left).

"Cioccio" (Vittorio Tortarolo) and his wife, Katia, on their wedding day, July 31, 1945.

Comando
1 Divisione d'assalto Garibaldi
G.BEVILACQUA

Prot. 30/235                              Zona d'impiego, 11 marzo 1945

Urgente

A TUTTI I COMANDI DIPENDENTI

Argomento : Comunicazione

　　　Si Trasmette la seguente comunicazione del Comando delle
Brigate d'Assalto "Garibaldi" -Delegazione Ligure- :
"Portiamo a conoscenza che in tutti i posti di blocco viene
adottato un nuovo sistema di allarme azionato a pedana.Ta-
le sistema permette al milite o al soldato di guardia ai
posti di blocco,pur con le mani alzate,di dare egualmente
l'allarme con la semplice pressione del piede. Prima di
intraprendere qualsiasi azione contro posti di blocco é indi-
spensabile procedere al taglio dei fili che collegano il
posto di blocco con il resto delle truppe. Tagliare i fili
uno per volta per non provocare il contatto e l'allarme."
　　　Si prega trasmettere quanto sopra ai Comandi di distaccamento alle dipendenza.

Il Commissario Politico                   Il Comandante Milit.

Military communication issued by the author (signature, lower right) informing his unit commanders that the enemy has equipped its checkpoints with emergency alarms that must be disabled before any attack is launched against them.

"Top secret" order for a meeting that the author received from the partisan high command, which he subsequently disobeyed.

Author at the May Day celebration in Savona, Italy, one week after the liberation of the city in 1945. *Right:* Standing in the main piazza of the city; the double star insignia on his uniform denotes the rank of lieutenant colonel. *Below:* Behind microphone, addressing assembled partisans from a second-floor balcony overlooking the main piazza; Colonel Zinnari is on his left.

Ceremonies marking the transfer of civil authority in Savona from partisan to regular Italian Army troops on May 8, 1945. *Above:* A mass held in the main piazza. Seated are disabled partisan veterans; standing at center (L to R): author (in leather jacket), Colonel Giorgio Salvi (commander of the regular army troops), the governor of the Province of Savona, and the mayor of the city of Savona. *Left:* Author and Colonel Salvi at the city's monument to the heroes of World War I.

# COMITATO DI LIBERAZIONE NAZIONALE
### CORPO VOLONTARIO DELLA LIBERTÀ

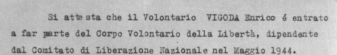

COMANDO 2a. ZONA LIGURE

Savona 17 Maggio 945

n° di prot. 1051

    Si atte sta che il Volontario VIGODA Enrico é entrato
a far parte del Corpo Volontario della Libertà, dipendente
dal Comitato di Liberazione Nazionale nel Maggio 1944.

    Successivamente gli fu affidato il Comando della
20° Brigata Garibaldina, che assunse in seguito la denomi=
nazione di 2a. Brigata, dislocata nella zona montana della
Provincia di Savona (Monte Sette Pani). Fu poi Comandante
della 4^ Brigata d'assalto Garibaldina Daniele Manin e nel
Febbraio 1945 fu nominato Comandante della Divisione d'assal=
to Garibaldina " Gin Bevilacqua", Comando che tenne fino al
25 Aprile 1945.

    Durante questo periodo partecipò a tutte le azioni
di guerra contro i nazifascisti, resistendo ai rastrellamen=
ti nemici, sopportando impavidamente i rigori della rigida
stagione invernale e comportandosi sempre da buon Partigiano.

IL COMMISSARIO DI GUERRA

V. MISTRANGELO

IL COMANDANTE

Col.R.ZINNARI

Document issued by the Committee of National Liberation certifying the author's role in the Italian partisan movement. The document reads, "Committee for National Liberation Voluntary Liberation Corps. *2d Ligurian Zone Headquarters.* Savona 17 May 1945. We certify that the Volunteer Enrico Vigoda joined the Voluntary Liberation Corps of the Committee for National Liberation in May 1944. Afterward he was given the command of the 20th Garibaldi Brigade, which was later named the 2d Brigade, located in the mountain area of the Savona province (Monte Sette Pani). He was then commander of the 4th Assault Brigade Daniele Manin, and in February 1945 he was appointed commander of the Garibaldi Assault Division "Gin Bevilacqua," a command that he held until 25 April 1945. During this time he participated in all war actions against the Nazi fascists, resisted the enemy, and bravely withstood the rigid winter season, always behaving as a good partisan."

Only once in the entire time of our sojourn in the mountains was it necessary to change the command of a unit because of improper behavior by the commander. I had instructed the officers not to order any personal services from the men or to accept them even if offered voluntarily. This order was issued because the entire partisan movement was based exclusively on voluntary service, and I had to see to it that a democratic system was strictly followed.

I never believed that it was necessary for the development of a good soldier to have him shine his commanding officer's shoes; to the contrary, I thought it was demoralizing and degrading. From my years of service as a young and quite rebellious lieutenant in the Polish armed forces, I considered such personal service a legacy of a now dead, archaic system of slavery. A similar system under the partisans was simply unthinkable. I expected every man, regardless of rank, myself included, to clean his own utensils and other belongings.

Thus it was unfortunate that I had to remove and reprimand one of my officers for his nonpartisan behavior. Victorio had been given the command of a detachment based on his military experience as a lieutenant in the former Italian army. He was a very energetic and capable man who was resolute and quite knowledgeable in military matters. His psychological capabilities, however, turned out to be nil. He carried on an old-style military regime in his camp, and the complaints multiplied until it became necessary to invoke the rules against him. So Comandante Victorio had to go before we lost the fidelity of the entire camp.

Initially we had only single-shot rifles, but as time went on and our contact with the enemy increased, so did our supply of automatic weapons. We simply ambushed the enemy and took what he had.

During the summer of 1944, our activities came to the attention of the Allied Command, and we were contacted by their representatives, a British major and an American officer. They offered us help in the form of military hardware and food, if and when necessary. What we needed most was ammunition for the different types of guns that we had captured from the Nazis and Fascists. We were continuously short of ammunition as a result of our heavy engagements with the enemy and of the continued influx of new men. The Allies were equally short of German ammunition, however, so they supplied us with British and American weapons instead. Together with the British and American officers, we developed a signal of lights, consisting of an X pattern set within a square, and thereby received supplies by airdrop at certain prearranged places in the mountains. If needed, the supplies came as often as every night and usually included automatic rifles, machine guns, 45-mm mortars, and always plenty of ammunition.

Later we acquired from the Allied command a great number of Sten guns. This British light submachine gun was the most efficient piece of automatic hardware we had on hand. These, along with somewhat less efficient German light submachine guns, were the best weapons for partisan use. With such a weapon, a man who was light on foot and had good agility, as well as a dose of courage, could perform miracles in the mountains, where topography was a partisan's best friend. For other types of battle, the rapid-firing German heavy machine gun was, we found, quite preferable to the slower, heavier British version.

After the war I was asked by many people, particularly British and American officers, how I managed to handle such a large group of heavily armed people without any disturbances. They wondered how I kept so many people scattered over such a large area under one unified command with no punitive facilities at hand. I was at a loss for answers to their questions. I had never given it a thought. The only thing I had promised my men was that with their help we would get rid of the enemy very soon.

Under such primitive conditions, it was an enormous, costly undertaking to supply such a large group of men with the bare necessities of life, but from the beginning we had agreed that the direct beneficiaries of the Fascist regime (most of whom, if not all, were very wealthy) should bear the responsibility for paying for the war. We were lucky to have a man among us who knew almost everyone in the Savona area. Logistics officer Little Mirto, as we called him, compiled a list of individuals of means who were still hanging on to their benefactor, Il Duce Mussolini, and his bankrupt ideas and who, out of necessity, collaborated with the Nazis. We then captured a few such individuals and kept them in temporary camps until they submitted to our demands; usually it took only a few short hours before they agreed to pay taxes to us for the purpose of maintaining the partisan movement. Once they submitted, we promptly released them unharmed. Shortly thereafter money, as well as clothing, shoes, and medicine, came in without a stop until the end of the war.

In the camps we had several physicians who performed miracles. In addition to caring for the men, they fought side by side with them as the occasion demanded. We were even able to place the sick and wounded in the city hospital right under the noses of the Nazis and their subservient slaves, the Fascists, because the local people were with us. One doctor in particular had been with us in the mountains from the beginning. Dr. Francesco Piana, known to us as Ivan, and his wife, Janina, had studied medicine together in Genoa. Janina—or Janinka, as I was privileged to call her—who was originally from Poland, did not quite make it through medical school because the unification of purpose between Hitler and his lackey Mussolini forced most foreigners out of Italian institutions of higher learning. But Janinka's medical knowledge did enable her to help her husband. Whereas Ivan was taciturn, Janinka was an extrovert, always ready with a reservoir of energy and a hearty smile. Ivan was almost continuously on the move, going up and down the mountains of the Savona area helping those who needed his attention. He not only provided medical help and secured hospitalization in the city but also furnished the necessary, often expensive, medicine without compensation. Ivan lived up to his Hippocratic oath, not just in lip service, but in honest deeds.

For all their efforts the men received no pay, and I am sure that as volunteers they expected none. We needed money only to buy food, which we acquired mostly from farmers or with their help. We paid for their goods and services promptly in cash, since those peasants were poor and could not afford to give away anything. I instructed the patrols roaming the area to stay away from the peasants' homes at all times. My reasoning behind the order was to protect the peasants from Nazi reprisals, as well from possible harassment from any misguided partisans (I wanted to ensure that drunk partisans would not be tempted to direct their power against the peasants instead of the enemy), and to protect my patrols from possible exposure to surprise enemy attacks. Largely because of this policy, we enjoyed the full cooperation of the people in our area at all times. Whenever a dubious individual managed to slip into our area, word of the event had a way of reaching me or the information officer immediately. For this reason, we had freedom of movement in our territory while the infiltration of enemies remained practically impossible. No partisan movement anywhere in the world can survive without the cooperation of the local population. The civilian population is the only entity with the means to keep the partisan informed and thereby enable him to inflict losses on the enemy as well as frustrate the enemy's plans to eliminate him. The Nazis and the Fascists could not understand how the bandits, as they called us, could dare to violently oppose the mightiest war machine in recorded history. They were equally blind to understanding a civilian population that staunchly supported the freedom fighters, even at the risk of losing their own lives in the process.

Only once did the actions of a partisan jeopardize our relationship with the peasants. Disregarding orders to the contrary, one of our young and capable partisans walked into a farmer's house and asked for some wine, which he was given. He then became drunk, grabbed the farmer's daughter, and raped her (fortunately, the farmer did not resist, since he would have been killed in the attempt to intervene). Then, apparently as an afterthought, the youth took some wool socks from a drawer before leaving.

Two days later we court-martialed the partisan and gave the farmer the opportunity to appear as witness for the prosecution. I assigned his entire detachment to serve as his jurors, and they sentenced him to death by firing squad. It was agonizing to have that boy executed, and I wished I could have avoided it, but it was necessary in order to make life safer for the multitude.

We got our information not only from the peasants but also from our own intelligence service, the Servizio Informazioni Militari, or SIM, which was in the exceptionally capable hands of a young man known as "Rosso." Although he had held a similar job with the Fascist regime, Rosso had been recommended to me by some of my friends who knew him well from before the war. They guaranteed his reliability. Indeed, Rosso performed exceeding well at the most delicate of all jobs. He organized a small group of collaborators for our side, planting them in the most sensitive places. He also established points of contact with our daily messengers for the purposes of transferring information and receiving orders. That service was interrupted only once, when one of our messengers was caught by the Nazis. The poor fellow would not talk, and the Nazis tortured him to death.

The result of the SIM service was that we always had an advance warning of any operation the enemy planned against us; sometimes the warning came as much as one full day ahead, but at others times we had only a few hours' notice. Nevertheless, we always had enough time to prepare an appropriate reception for the enemy, denying him the element of surprise. In such encounters the enemy, stopped before he was ready to fight, was sent back down to the valley with a bloody nose, so to speak. Using this tactic, we gained more German equipment than we could possibly use.

We also took great care to safeguard our security from within. With few exceptions, each group was composed entirely of men from the same locale, all of whom knew one another and many of whom were even related. This system of organization prevented us from being infiltrated by enemy spies, a practice at which the Nazis were masters, particularly when they had plenty of volunteers from among the low-lying Fascists.

One thing we failed to achieve throughout the war was a balanced diet for the men. We did have sporadic improvements, however. For example, from one ambushed convoy we netted French cognac and various Italian wines, as well as German wine and brandy. Since that particular convoy consisted of horse-drawn wagons, we also remained burdened with a score of Belgian horses. At first we did not know what to do with them, but Mirto suggested that horse meat broiled in olive oil would make a good dish. We killed a few of the horses for our own consumption and traded the rest to farmers for sheep and piglets.

During another attack on an enemy convoy, near the town of Calizzano, we managed to confiscate three heavy trucks loaded with five-pound cans of tuna fish, as well as other food and merchandise. For months we ate tuna fish twice daily. That particular ambush developed into a tenacious fight because the Nazis, not realizing that they had no chance, decided to make a stand. After the better part of two hours, it was all over. We lost two good men in the process of killing a dozen Nazis and capturing six others. It goes without saying that we could not afford to keep any prisoners.

# 14 Negotiations with a German Commander

My command post was located in a cave high up in the mountains. On the Mediterranean side, the Germans had a base in the valley of Vado-Ligure, which served as our main supply route. The only way the Nazis could have reached us would have been by foot, through a steep, narrow path that could hold only one man at a time. To our rear, and also in a valley, was a unit of the San Marco Division of the reborn Fascist army.

The San Marco unit was equipped with a 155-mm battery that they used on us nightly. Although we were separated by nearly twelve miles of winding mountain roads, the straight-line distance between us was just over a mile. Each night those artillery shells flew up to us for an hour, after which they fell silent. That was the signal for us to return the fire with our 81-mm mortars, using the sound of their artillery to direct our own fire. Afterward there invariably was a lull until the next evening. Such seesaw shelling had no effect whatsoever on either side.

We employed mortar shells for other purposes as well, such as mining the approaches to our camps. We profusely mined all the paths important enough to be shown on military maps. The mines did not explode automatically; rather, they used a relatively simple detonation system we developed. Under the personal supervision of our pyrotechnic, Ernesto, our special squad would place several serially connected mortar shells, coupled with plastic explosive of Allied origin, at intervals of several meters in a strategically selected spot, usually in a heavily wooded area. The detonation of the mines was relatively safe and required only one man to operate the generator. The generator was located a considerable distance from the area in which we expected the enemy attack but still close enough for the man in charge to keep the enemy under visual contact. Thus, he was able to evaluate the situation and decide when to press the button to achieve the most devastating effect. The man in charge waited until the enemy column was centered over the charge before releasing that terrible force, which created havoc in the enemy formation.

In addition to being our main source of supplies, the town of Vado-Ligure later became important for another reason. In the beginning, when our forces were insignificant, the Nazis did not bother to save our men as prisoners. Called outlaws or bandits, we were treated as such, or worse, and when the Nazis caught our men, they first tortured and then killed them. We in turn had no facilities for prisoners of war and promptly dispatched those taken alive, although we did not indulge in torture of any kind.

In time, however, as we grew in number and became better organized and better armed, the situation changed considerably. Our movements began to be free from Nazi interference, while the reverse became true for the enemy; our actions against them partially restricted their movements. The Nazis became aware, albeit slowly, of our changed position and recognized that perhaps we were more than just bandits. From that time on, whenever they captured any of our men, we quickly captured and held onto some of theirs. In negotiations for an exchange of prisoners with the Nazis, we engaged the services of the local Catholic priest from the Vado-Ligure parish. Padre Giovanni served as mediator for both sides. At first reluctant, the Nazis soon learned to adjust themselves to the idea that they were no longer the sole masters of the area.

I had met the padre sometime before while I was on an inspection tour. He had been on his way to see a sick person when we stopped him to make sure he was a priest. None of the men with me knew him, and priest's clothing meant little under war conditions. To verify his claim, we accompanied him to his destination, and needless to say, he turned out to be the person he claimed to be. Padre Giovanni ended up being my good friend through the rest of the war. As a priest he was interested in the spiritual well-being of the boys in the mountains, especially since the men were mostly of local stock and thus primarily Catholics. There were in fact few exceptions, such as a few German deserters, who were Lutherans, and a few Yugoslavs, who I believe were Greek Orthodox. We also had one or perhaps two Russians who claimed no religious affiliation. And, of course, there was myself.

The good padre suggested, and I agreed, that some religion in the form of a field mass could do no harm. I also thought it might even improve the continuous morale of our partisans, at least for some of them. In organizing such an affair, however, we confronted a few major problems, namely how, where, and when to hold mass. While we all agreed that it would be quite imposing for such a sizable group of men to assemble in one large place with a solemn atmosphere, listening to the chant of a holy mass, we had the men's safety to consider. Finally it was agreed that we would grant the padre the privilege of holding a mass but that not all the men would take part at the same time. The location was to be the plateau that we were using to receive airdrops from the Allies, and the brigade to participate first would the fourth, which at that time was fairly close. We also invited the nearby peasants to participate. Of course, all the necessary precautions were taken so that we would not be surprised by an enemy attack.

I was pleased with the outcome of the event. In a partisan movement, any event not directly related to battle is of a voluntary nature, and in this particular case, no one was compelled to participate in the mass. It was therefore amazing to watch all those boys flock to the service. A few days later we had one more mass for the rest of the men, and everything worked out fine.

The padre's most difficult job as negotiator came in the later part of October 1944, after one of our night patrols was caught in an ambush. Three good, experienced men were captured, so we were puzzled but never found out how that could have happened. That morning I sent my special squad, which we had named "the Gappisti," down the valley to capture a Nazi, preferably an officer. I put Il Tigre, commander of the Rebagliati detachment, in charge of that group.

It was not long before my men came up the mountains with a captain who could hardly speak from exhaustion when he was finally brought to me. I gave him some time to rest. Then I explained why he had suddenly found himself in the mountains among the rebels and politely apologized for the inconvenience. I told him that no harm would come to him as long as our men held prisoners by the Nazi authorities likewise were unharmed. Finally, I explained that he was simply a hostage for the release of our men.

My frame of mind generally precluded any pity when dealing with Nazis, but sometimes there were exceptions to the rule. I felt sorry for that fellow, who was the father of five. But this was a cruel war. That night we secured the prisoner and rested.

I knew that the captain would be missed almost immediately, so we expected to hear something from the German command in the near future. As anticipated, the padre came to see us early the next morning. Excitedly he told us that he had been summoned to the German command in Savona because they claimed that the captain had been caught in Vado-Ligure, which was the padre's jurisdiction. The Nazis had arrested ten citizens from his parish as hostages and had given him twenty-four hours to produce the captain or face the consequences.

I told the padre that we did indeed have the officer and proposed that he take a message from me to the Nazi command. I addressed that message "to whom it may concern" at the German headquarters in Savona. Their missing officer, I wrote, was in our hands; he was tired but otherwise well. I explained that we had captured him to trade for our men whom they had in custody, and I assured them that actions such as the taking of innocent civilians from the valley as hostages would not speed the return of their officer. I threatened to execute their officer immediately if any of the hostages or our men were harmed. Also included was a warning that any attempt to free the officer by force would not meet with success. I signed that message with my formal title: "Enrico, Commander of the Fourth Brigade of the Garibaldi, Province of Savona."

We did not have to wait long for an answer. Late that same afternoon the poor padre was back with a reply from the German commander in Savona. The correspondence was in German, of course, so only the padre and I were able to read it. In his first message written to an avowed bandit, the Nazi commander flatly refused to negotiate any exchange with us on the basis of thirteen for one.

I worked late that night by the light of a candle, writing in longhand since my secretary did not know German and I was a poor typist. The German commander's letter to me also had been written in longhand, but I doubt it was a lack of secretarial help that had prompted such discretion in his dealings with a bandit. In my answer to his letter, I suggested that the exchange ratio that he found so terribly unfair was by no means my idea; it was, rather, a system introduced by his fellow Nazis in the occupied countries of Europe, where often the imposed ratio was much higher. I further informed him that his total contempt for human rights, as demonstrated by his hasty action in the Vado community, made it sufficiently clear that fairness and justice were empty words when uttered by a Nazi.

Several days later a message arrived from the commander demanding, as before, a one-for-one exchange. I began to consider our correspondence an exercise in futility and did not send a reply. Meanwhile, Rosso, our SIM officer, reported an increase in both the Italian and German military forces in the area, a situation requiring our immediate and undivided attention. Apparently they were preparing for something, but Rosso was unable to get any solid information because the incoming forces were largely uncommunicative. I then was informed that other mixed forces were being concentrated in the area of Calizzano, to our rear. It thus became obvious that we were the objects of their attention.

Clearly, our prisoner had to be kept at all cost, so I sent him, under a selected heavy guard, in the general direction of St. Bernardino, a mountain pass between Imperia and Cuneo. Our men would have fewer problems guarding him at that much higher elevation. Then I kept myself busy taking the necessary precautions to prepare for an unknown factor. We doubled the guards and increased the patrols. We also prepared bases of operation further up on higher ground in case we were forced to retreat or otherwise temporarily give up some ground.

After several days of not hearing from the padre (which was disturbing, to say the least), he came running up to my cave and told me that the German commander had agreed to guarantee my safe conduct, as well as my safe return, if I agreed to meet him anywhere in Savona. His sudden proposal was rather unusual, but I could see nothing wrong with such as meeting, provided it would help bring the boys back. I countered his proposal by suggesting a meeting in the Vado-Ligure area instead of in Savona. I would let him select the time, but I reserved the choice of the place. The following day he informed me that he agreed to my terms.

I selected a little bridge in Vado, not far from the foot of the mountains and just outside a row of houses. Our meeting and conference would be on the center of that bridge, and I accepted the selection of the padre as a neutral party in this unusual encounter. I gave orders to secure both ridges of the Vado-Ligure valley, and I put two of our best men in charge of the operation. As yet I did not know the day or hour of the meeting. That evening the padre informed me that the German wished to meet me the following day at 1:30 in the afternoon. I promptly agreed. The padre, sure that he would not have to come for any other instructions, said that he hoped to see me the next day at the agreed time and place.

The patrols on the ridges over Vado reported that they noticed some military movements in the vicinity of Via Aurellia coming in their general direction and that they had exchanged a few minutes of small-arms fire. After that, there were no more disturbances.

The next day, of course, was important for every one of us. It was to be my first, and as it turned out my last, experience of such a delicate nature. Aware that many things could go wrong, I knew that there was only a slim chance that I would come out of it alive. How ironic it would have been finally to be killed now that the end of that terrible war could almost be seen. There was a feeling in the air that the Nazis were on their last legs, and it would have been pitiful indeed to lose out when the climax was quickly approaching.

The distance from my cave to that little bridge took approximately an hour and a half to cross on foot (to measure mountain distances in miles could be deceiving). We left the cave about 11:30, deliberately walking slowly down the mountain so that I would not be too tired for the encounter. Confrontation with an enemy during a war is in itself a serious matter, and I believed that the prerequisite for success was restful alertness. We timed our walk so we would be a few minutes late and arrive when they were already there.

As I approached the bridge, I saw only two men. I recognized one as the padre, and the other had to be the German officer. He had stationed a German jeep with a machine gun and five men about 150 yards or so away, in the middle of the road. All his men were armed with submachine guns, but as we had agreed, he was unarmed.

The German turned out to be a naval officer who was the assistant commander of the Savona garrison. He was very polite and his behavior quite correct. Initially our conversation was strictly formal, but in a short time we began to shed some of the formality and agreed on the time and place for the prisoner exchange. The officer, under the impression that I was a misguided German, then suggested that I follow him and help them with the war effort for the glory of the Reich. I responded by inviting him to leave his troops and join the partisan cause. The agreed time and place for the final exchange was to be two days hence near Calizzano on the road leading to Savona. Our men and the hostages taken in Vado were to be let free in advance of the captain. The officer and I parted in a rather friendly manner with the conventional wishes of good luck and a handshake.

On reaching the first mountain range on our return to camp after meeting with the German officer, we received the disturbing news that our *staffetta* had not reported back to camp that day. I sent the reserve man down to Nola to place a telephone call to Rosso in Savona. Nola was another place we used for information and direct contact with Savona. Rosso asked our reserve man to wait for him in the usual place, a small church courtyard toward the foot of the mountain. Rosso met with the man and reported that he had given our usual *staffetta* the news that either the next day or the day after that, the Nazis would attack our area in force with several battalions each of San Marco and German mountaineers, as well as Camicie Nere (Fascist Blackshirts) and German infantry. Rosso was certain that our *staffetta* had been caught; otherwise, he would have been either in camp or in Savona.

This was not the first extermination action that the Nazis had launched against us. Although they always used a ratio of twenty to one in their favor, they had never been able to achieve their objective. After such actions, the Nazis usually issued a communique claiming total victory, having rid the entire area of bandits. The truth was, of course, that they were usually beaten and forced to leave in a hurry, while we continued to grow and expand. But this time, judging by the number of forces being concentrated against us, their effort promised to be greater. We were always on standby, an essential prerequisite for our continuous ability to fight, and with this latest emergency, we simply increased our vigilance. The auxiliary bases we had scattered all over our mountainous area prevented the Nazis from employing a strategy of surprise and encirclement. Still, no one could ever predict the final outcome of a battle.

It was November 28, 1944. That evening, after I gave the staff a report of my meeting with the German officer and following a short discussion, we went for a final inspection of the camp periphery. We could detect nothing unusual. Every man was alert at his post, perhaps a little more so for having heard the latest news of the intensive concentration of enemy forces down in the valley.

The Fourth Brigade, which I was commanding at the time, was encamped in a strategically favorable area around Monte Alto, Piano dei Corsi, and San Giacomo overlooking Savona, Vado-Ligure, and the bay. The only place we never occupied was Monte Alto itself, a somewhat cone-shaped giant of a mountain. As the tallest mountain in the immediate vicinity, it was the most vulnerable and most untenable position to hold.

We assumed our area would be the one most likely selected by the enemy for a major attack. We had three detachments of approximately one hundred men each in the immediate vicinity, plus my command post. We were well armed and in high spirits. We were advised by the regional command in Genoa to try to keep our commander and his assistant in separate places at all times to avoid endangering the command structure. I also had a standing order from them that under no circumstances should I personally take part in any action, but I felt that I could not just look on when my friends were fighting.

While inspecting the area that evening, we suddenly heard the sound of one of our machine guns coming from a ridge overlooking the bay area. Later it was reported to me that the gun was manned by Diego, one of our best men. At just about the same time, the rapid bursts of a German machine gun and some small-arms fire were clearly distinguishable. The Nazis were also using small mortars in the attack.

With the advent of daylight, the battle developed into a full-scale military operation. Already it was apparent that any strategy would be ours alone, for the attacking enemy was forced to adapt to conditions beyond his control. Our movements remained unrestricted in all places throughout the entire battle.

During their initial deployment, the enemy did manage to take Monte Alto, where they set up their radio communication equipment. As soon as that was discovered, however, our Gappisti, together with an assault squad led by my old friend, the sergeant whom I had freed from the Corso-Rici jail, moved in and completely destroyed the German command post. The lack of communications rendered the enemy's situation untenable and enabled us to turn to a full offensive. We attacked in small groups from every possible angle, and at the same time we used our strategically placed heavy machine guns and 81-mm mortars to block the few avenues through which they could either escape or receive reinforcements.

Toward the late afternoon of November 29, one could observe Fascists everywhere running away in confusion, ahead of the Nazis, like rats from a sinking ship. I could not resist the temptation to participate directly in this spectacular event. Our special squad, using automatic guns and hand grenades, flushed the enemy out from their well-prepared attack positions into the path of our mortars and machine guns, as well as into the mine fields that we had prepared in advance. They could not use artillery against us, since the quarters were too close; otherwise they would have fired from their positions in the valleys surrounding us. Even their airplane that circled us for a while was of no help to them, since its radio calls to Monte Alto were sent to a communication center that we had already destroyed.

It was just about twilight when the Germans increased the pace of their retreat. I sent into action against the retreating enemy the same groups that had protected me during my conference with the German officer. Our boys took an extra heavy toll of them, mainly in wounded. As night approached, all was quiet up in the mountains, and only the faint staccato of small-arms fire could be heard coming from way down in the valleys. Slowly the men began returning to their respective bases.

It took the rest of that night and the greater part of the next day to assess the result of the memorable fight. Losses on our side were five dead and six wounded. We assumed that the enemy losses were greater, since there were more of them and their effort was colossal. The most important fact, of course, was that the enemy had not achieved their major objective: the destruction of the partisan movement. In fact, they had not even managed to dislodge us from our positions. To top it off, it was they who left the battlefield in disarray.

The enemy offensive had not been against our brigade alone; it had included simultaneous attacks against the Third, Fifth, and Sixth Brigades as well. On the second day after the battle, news began to come in from the other fronts: the Sixth Brigade apparently had no contact with the enemy after they moved to higher ground; the other two brigades came out well, despite their lack of space in which to maneuver, and managed to contain the enemy and fight from fixed positions, a strategy for which the enemy was unprepared. After some limited action, the enemy moved on. Subsequently we were informed that the enemy losses from all three places of engagement totaled eighty-seven men dead or wounded. They left fourteen of their dead behind, providing us with fourteen pairs of good shoes, for which we always had need.

We barely had managed to settle down after that memorable engagement when my friend the padre showed up again. I was now aware that the Nazi officer had known quite well what was in store for us when he had talked with me on that little bridge in Vado. He must have thought that having seen the mysterious commander of mountain bandits, he would be able to pick me out from among the other partisans who would soon be taken prisoner.

The padre informed me that our men and the ten hostages were still in German hands, and I retained him for the rest of the day. Then I sent him down with a written message demanding the immediate release of the civilians before I would resume negotiations. At the same time, I sent our Gappisti down into the valley to bring up a couple more Germans. They returned the same evening with a lieutenant and two enlisted men.

In the meantime I prepared another message to the Nazi commander. I demanded one hundred pairs of new shoes, warm underwear, and wool socks for the approaching winter. In that letter I included messages written by the captive Nazis to show that our prisoners were alive and well. I gave him twenty-four hours to comply with our demands. He responded promptly, asking for the reinstatement of the original agreement made before the attack, except for the necessary rescheduling of time. I, of course, refused. After that, the German commander of Savona accepted all the conditions imposed by me in full. Never before in my career had I received as much satisfaction as I did from that transaction.

The memorable fight of November 1944 was the last of the major engagements in the partisan war with the Nazis. With the realization that destroying the partisan forces, at least in the Savona area, was a mathematical impossibility, the Germans gave up trying. Small, but sometimes fierce, skirmishes continued practically nonstop until the snow slowed them to sporadic affairs.

Shortly after that November engagement, I was approached by the command of the Seconda Zona di Ligure in Genoa with a request—or rather, an order—to unite the four brigades under their jurisdiction into a division over which I was to assume command. By then it was on record that the only unit that remained completely intact and did not retreat before the enemy during the November fight was the Fourth Brigade. I believed it was unfair, however, to ascribe the successful conclusion of that battle only to our virtue, for factors such as location and topography had played major roles in our success. The order, written by Colonel Zinnari himself, directing me to organize a division from the scattered remnants of the other three brigades, was unusually vague, and thus it gave me broad latitude. This was the manner in which I was appointed commander of an as yet nonexistent division.

It was a rather tedious job to put the small groups together, for they were scattered over approximately 650 square kilometers. To begin with, I decided to inspect all the units personally. My direct contact, I believe, had a salutary effect on the men in the different brigades, as well as on their respective commanders. With the fame of the Fourth Brigade preceding us, we were received with great enthusiasm everywhere we went. This was also the first time that we traveled on the road for more than a week without being pestered by the enemy.

On the return to our cave after the inspection tour, we were caught in the first snow of the season. For me, walking up and down mountain trails covered with light snow was a new experience, for I was no mountaineer. Although the warm ground caused the snow to melt quickly, it also produced mud, which hampered our movements and consequently slowed us down.

Back at the command post we were greeted with an unexpected development—a rapid influx of hundreds of volunteers, mainly deserters from Mussolini's San Marco Division. This created an unusual security problem, since these men until recently had been collaborating with the enemy. But they also were Italians.

We simply were in no position to investigate them, since they were from all over Italy. The guidance we requested from the zone command was unsatisfactory, and we were burdened with a lot of wasted time spent trying to weed out the undesirable elements. We discovered some spies that the Nazis had planted among the new arrivals. Even some of the San Marco officers sought contact with me on several occasions. After meeting with them a few times, however, I had to classify them as not proper material for the mountains, particularly among us rebels. I ordered them to stay where they were, and instead of letting them join us, I demanded that they promise to help us block the Nazis' eventual retreat from the area. I made this order so as to keep the Germans in the area from slipping out to join up with other Nazis in the Po valley. As it later turned out, the San Marco officers failed to keep that promise. I also demanded that they furnish us with all the supplies we needed, a demand to which they promptly agreed without protest. They even went as far as to propose that at the proper time they would deliver their commanding general into our hands.

I was officially not an Italian, but I felt very much like one, which automatically precluded any built-in hatred on my side for those confused San Marco deserters, regardless of whom they had once served. For some reason I could never equate two individuals such as Hitler and Mussolini. I believed Mussolini to be more humane. Although I knew little if anything about Fascists before coming to Italy, after I arrived and learned the language, I gained the impression that they were quite hated by the people and already on their way out. Prior to arriving in Italy, however, I was already familiar with three of Mussolini's ill-fated international adventures: his stupid escapade in Ethiopia, his silly efforts to help Franco in the Spanish civil war, and his foolish attempt to help Hitler in France. The last, I believe, was a reflection of an obsession with his assumed greatness, which gained him only disrespect and justifiable hatred from the Italian people.

At that time I was not aware of any extermination camps, or for that matter any concentration camps, established by the Fascists inside or outside their country. I also had not heard of the existence of any Italian slave labor camps like the notorious ones that the Nazis had established all over occupied Europe. But some of my partisans had personal matters to settle with the Camicie Nere or with outright informers. I always had a particular distaste for informers, who worked to the ruin of the people for the sole purpose of material gain. I never could reconcile such a thing.

In addition to a rapid influx of deserters from the San Marco Division, there came an increasing number of civilians who began to discern the end of the Nazi-Fascist rule. But something entirely different also occurred. We were joined by some young girls from Savona. At first there were only four girls, but more came later. Some of them had been active underground fighters whose assignments had been quite dangerous. When the enemy discovered their activity, they had no choice but to leave their homes and seek safety in the mountains with us.

I did what I considered best under the circumstances. I assigned the girls a separate enclave and had a tent erected for them. When I ordered Little Mirto to see that the girls had the necessary means of protection, he issued them small arms and gave them basic instructions in handling pistols. In addition, we placed a guard in front of their tent at night.

There was one girl in particular who aroused everyone's attention. Her name was Fulvia. I had my reservations about admitting her into the partisan fold, but the recommendation of the local command of the Savona partisans convinced me that her presence was quite justified. She was barely fifteen years old, but already she was a major criminal in the eyes of the local Nazis. According to the report I received on her, she had been a member of the local partisan movement charged with putting up anti-Nazi and anti-Fascist slogans printed by the Committee of National Liberation. Girls like Fulvia also were adept at painting slogans on sidewalks; they used the same type of phosphorous paint used by the Nazis to illuminate the curbs at street crossings at night. I remember seeing those anti-Nazi slogans on the sidewalks while I was still active in Savona, but at the time I did not know who the masters of that endeavor were.

The report stated that a group of four girls was ambushed during a slogan-writing episode. Three of them managed to get away in the dark of the night. The one they arrested was a lookout who had warned the others without leaving herself time to escape. That poor girl broke down under torture and gave them the names of the other girls. Meanwhile Fulvia, after escaping, had gone to the home of a family friend, avoiding her own home. The next day, after learning of the lookout's arrest, she thought it wise to stay where she was and inform the local partisan command of her whereabouts. Such were the contents of the report given to me after Fulvia suddenly appeared in our camp. I would call her "little Fulvia," but one should not use the term *little* when talking about Fulvia. Those who did not know her would assume her to be a full-grown woman. She was essentially a child, however, albeit not a spoiled one.

For their protection, I ordered the girls to higher ground during major engagements with the enemy. The only one who protested such a distinction was Fulvia, who insisted on the right to stay with the men and fight, arguing and begging for the opportunity. She was already quite knowledgeable in handling arms, a knowledge I believe she acquired from the partisan group in Savona while under their guidance. Against my better judgment, I decided to let her join in the fighting alongside other partisans and assigned her to a machine-gun squad. The leader of the squad later reported that her performance during battle was excellent in every respect. In the days that followed I included her on inspection tours to help us give pep talks to the men.

Being a close witness to the performance of women under duress, I recalled the opinion of a man well-known to all the boys in the mountains. I had in mind, of course, Benito Mussolini, whose theory was that women were created for the sole purpose of bearing children and taking care of the kitchen. Those young Italian girls who took up arms and fought for freedom side by side with the most courageous of men in the mountains of Italy demonstrated to the domestic Fascists, as well as to their masters, the Nazis, the stupidity of their theory about women. Right after the war, those heroic Italian girls had the unusual satisfaction of seeing the author of such theories, the man who almost brought their beautiful country to ruin, dangling from the hook of a filthy gas station in Milan with his mistress at his side.

The Italian women had a relatively short but hard struggle. Their contribution to the war of liberation was significant. The largest credit by far has to go to those women in the cities who daily risked their lives to liberate their country from the hated enemy from abroad as well as from his foolish followers within.

# 15 Execution of a Nazi

Although we were under the overall command of the Committee of National Liberation, we had plenty of latitude, and I had full freedom of action, including the power over life and death. No one ever questioned my authority in matters of command. Still, in cases dealing with the Fascists, I always saw to it that impartiality was the rule rather than the exception; for such cases we had a duly instituted court of law staffed by attorneys and some young students of law at the University of Genoa. But I reserved the exclusive right to deal with the Nazis myself. As far as the Nazis were concerned, I had not a shred of pity left. I knew only to do with Nazis what the Nazis had done to innocent people all over Europe for the last several years. I had witnessed many of their actions personally, and I knew there were important differences between us. I did not kill indiscriminately. I never tortured anyone.

At times of winter calm, when the snow hampered our activities, I resorted to deep contemplation. I tried to think carefully about myself and about the value of life itself, which was lost to me at times. The term *death*, which has been referred to as "Majesty," lost every meaning for me, except when I was capable of applying it in conjunction with the term *Nazi*. Then, and only then, did death have a meaning for me, inasmuch as it helped to carry out an act of justice against the killers of innocent children.

At times such thoughts frightened me. I wondered what it would be like after all this came to an end, when I again would be a free man in a peaceful world. Would that cynical view of life remain with me?

These were the questions turning in my mind when I was awakened to reality by the loud, clear voice of Sergeant Noce reporting that he and a few of his men had been in a fight that morning in the area of Altare. He thought that they had killed several Nazis, and he had brought back some prisoners as well. They were being kept in an old shack halfway down the mountain from our cave. This was one of the small shacks used by tenant farmers to keep their chestnut tree leaves, which we used for mattresses or, in times of shortage (which was most of the time), for tobacco. Those secluded shacks were ideal places to keep prisoners for interrogation and for final disposition.

When I arrived, the prisoners were secured inside the shack. Two of them were very young boys. The third was a middle-aged fellow who was a little on the heavy side. We started the interrogation with the two boys first. As soon as they uttered a few words, it was apparent that they were not Germans. Both were from Katowice, which was a major industrial hub in Gorny-Slask, a part of Poland ceded by the Germans at the end of World War I.

The boys had been picked up during a *Razzia* in which the Nazis had everyone found within an area of several city blocks forcibly hauled away in heavy trucks for processing. The processing consisted of separating the able-bodied from the old and disabled. The Nazis then shipped the young ones to special camps where they were turned into German soldiers, who were then sent to different parts of Nazi-occupied Europe to serve in the Wehrmacht. This was how the Germans refilled the by then depleted ranks of their beaten armies. After being grabbed by the Nazis, the boys were not even given the opportunity to notify their parents of their whereabouts. They were sent to Krakow, where they were fully equipped in German uniforms, given a few weeks' training as well as instruction in the German language, and then shipped off for service in Italy.

Such prisoners were considered friends. We immediately incorporated them into our units. Since I was the only one who could understand them, I kept them close to our command post at the Fourth Brigade.

The other prisoner was another matter altogether. He was an officer, and therefore I had to scrutinize him quite carefully. After a lengthy interrogation, I was almost ready to believe that he was a decent fellow. Then I was given some photographs found on him. They depicted scenes of executions from different areas in eastern Europe, and in each our captive lieutenant appeared to be the man in charge of the hangings. There were usually several Nazis around those gallows, but he was the one who had issued the orders. He had been so methodical as to write the dates and locations of these macabre feats on the backs of the pictures. Recorded there were the names "Russia," "Lithuania," "Latvia," and "Estonia."

I glanced at him without uttering a word. He was ashen. There he was, the haughty Nazi, now a bundle of misery. When I finally managed to put a question to him, he barely opened his mouth and mumbled something that I understood to mean "justice."

I was not quite sure that I had heard him properly, so I repeated my question, asking him to explain the meaning of those executions. It took him quite a while to raise his head, thereby indicating that he had regained his composure. I expected that he might, like so many others we had confronted in similar situations, claim that he only had been following orders. Without hesitation, in a typical Prussian staccato style, he tried to explain to me the reason for the different hangings. Justice, he said to me, had to be done to the bandits who were disturbing the peaceful life of the communities of which he had been in charge. Under the circumstances, I was almost certain that he had lost his mind by even thinking that such an answer would sway me.

As I was trying to decide what to do next, he fell on his knees in front of me. He begged me to please have pity on his three little children and wife, who were now living in Altona in northern Germany with his ill mother. His sudden action sent a feeling of sickening disgust through me. I turned away from him and gave orders to follow the usual procedure in cases where Nazis were involved. Then I went back to my cave in the mountains.

In all candor, I have to admit that even if I had possessed the facilities necessary to maintain a prisoner-of-war camp, the Nazis would definitely have been excluded from such camps. In my opinion, the Nazis were not entitled to any benefit derived from international law or any other custom practiced by civilized people anywhere in the world.

# 16    We Liberate Savona

Through the years we lost quite a few men, by far the great majority on the field of battle. But it is something else again when men are lost by default.

Two brothers, Pasquale and Stefano Figuccio, known as "Jim" and "Stiv," were with us in the winter of 1944–45. Jim was twenty-five years old and Stiv was nineteen. I had met and inherited Jim the day I took over command of the Calcagno detachment. Prior to the war he was a chemistry student in his senior year. When I met him he was the detachment's secretary, and I made a sound judgment to continue him in that role. He was a highly intelligent and exceptionally friendly young man, qualities that helped to cement the close friendship that developed between us. My job entailed a great deal of written matter, especially the daily correspondence to and from Savona. Jim was most helpful in supplementing my linguistic shortcomings with his superior intelligence. As soon as I uttered a couple of sentences, he promptly anticipated the rest, and invariably the finished product was a masterpiece of classical eloquence. Sometimes I felt that he could read my mind.

Stiv learned of me from Jim, and from the time he joined us he looked up to me as if I too were his older brother.

Against my better judgment, I gave Jim permission to visit his parents during Christmastime at their home in Celle-Ligure, but without his younger brother. I always kept the two brothers separated and never allowed them to participate in the same mission, so that only one of them would be exposed to danger at a time. But Stiv continued to beg me to let him go with Jim, and I relented. I have regretted that moment of weakness ever since. On January

20, 1945, the day they were to return to camp, the brothers were ambushed and killed by the enemy. For a long time after their assassination by the Nazis, I blamed myself for losing them, since it had been in my power to prevent them from going home. Only five short months later, that most terrible of all wars would be over.

On February 1, 1945, twelve days after that tragic event, the four brigades were officially formed into a new division, and I was appointed its commander. We named ourselves the 1ª Divisione d'Assalto Garibaldi "Gin Bevilacqua" (1st Gin Bevilacqua Garibaldi Assault Division) in honor of a freedom fighter of great renown whose battle name had been "Leone." Leone had been the political commissioner of the Calcagno detachment when I assumed its command and later served in the same capacity with the Fifth Brigade. He was captured and then killed by the Nazis two months prior to the formation of the new division.

After losing Jim, I appointed Cioccio, an able bookkeeper from Savona, as secretary. In the performance of their jobs, Cioccio and Jim were similar in efficiency, but there was a difference between the two that was hard to characterize. Jim was sophisticated, a young intellectual of high standards, whereas Cioccio was hard working, intelligent, and friendly. Cioccio had a girlfriend, Katia, who was only sixteen at the time. She could not come up into the mountains to visit Cioccio, and he could not go down to visit her in the valley unescorted. But the ingenuity of a woman, even a sixteen-year-old girl, and the strong magnet of love were capable of performing miracles. Katia acted against the Nazis in a way that made it unsafe for her to stay at home or even in the community, so she had to escape to the mountains. Katia thus popped up suddenly in our midst and was placed in the small camp with the other girls. She and Cioccio later exchanged vows in a church in the valley during a ceremony officiated by none other than our famous and heroic Padre Giovanni. I was one of the guests and also served as one of the two official witnesses.

One month after the establishment of our new division, in March 1945, I received a message to meet with our Allied agent at my convenience, but as soon as possible, to receive some secret information that he had to turn over to me personally. Our contact man with the Allied authorities, Piero, was an employee of the British Military Mission in eastern Liguria. I met with him halfway down the mountain the following day.

The information I received was that the Nazis had supposedly agreed to surrender on April 25, and my group was to be ready to march down to the cities on that date. The agent also had a personal admonition for me to be cautious, since right after the war there was likely to be a squabble for power, and I might get caught in the middle of it. My contact indicated that although he served as an Allied agent, he was nevertheless an Italian and as such was familiar with the local situation. At the time I did not quite understand what he was trying to tell me, but I knew that it had something to do with Italian politics.

The Committee of National Liberation was composed of a variety of parties, including the Christian Democratic Party, the Liberal Party, two different socialist parties, the Center Party, and the Communist Party. It was, in short, a conglomeration of different parties from the extreme left to right, with the exclusion of the Fascists and the Monarchists. I stayed clear of direct involvement in any of these political groupings, which I considered to be solely the province of my Italian friends. My interest in Italy, which was strictly personal, was to fight the Nazi brutes and not much else.

On April 18, 1945, a letter came from the general headquarters in Genoa signed by Inspector Simon, the same gentleman who had originally asked me to assume command of the partisan group in the Savona area. The letter, dated April 16, was marked "TOP SECRET" and was addressed to me personally. I was ordered to take to the road immediately to join other division commanders of the Genoa Region for an important regional meeting that was to take place at the headquarters of the Sixth Zone Command located near Genoa. The order also stated that I was to go to the camp of the Mingo Division, which had already been given orders to take me through the mountains. Furthermore, the Mingo Division was to furnish me with a guide who would take me to the command of the Sixth Zone. Finally, the order authorized my second in command, Vice Comandante Radomir, to take over in my absence. The projected reunion of the commanders would take place on April 20, only two days away. I was told to make all necessary haste, even do the impossible, to arrive on time.

Without giving it a second thought, I was ready to follow the order. I summoned Radomir and gave him instructions for assuming temporary command during my few days' absence. Then I relaxed and began to compare dates and events. I contemplated the distance I would have to traverse over mountains and valleys to reach my destination, as per the order. An important factor to consider was my knowledge of the outlying area, which was zero. The farthest point east of Savona with which I was familiar was the mountain above Celle-Ligure.

I also tried to find a logical explanation for the importance of such a meeting in the light of the events now rapidly approaching. If there were special problems to discuss, could they not be outlined in a written order just as well? The prospect of being led by an unknown guide forty kilometers or more over mountains, across highways already clogged with retreating Nazis, and through territory with which I was unfamiliar while not knowing or being known by anyone did not particularly appeal to me. The more I thought about the idea, the less I liked it. Although there was no tangible reason to be suspicious, I began to feel the same restlessness that had saved my life in Poland. Perhaps the admonition I had received from the Allied agent Piero contributed to my state of mind. But when I compared the date of the order and the date I received it with the date by which I was to arrive, I knew it was absolutely impossible for me to comply. Even if I had wanted to, I could not have made it on time.

The date of April 25 and the expected Nazi surrender were continuously before my eyes. With only a few short days left until the end of the war and victory over the Nazis, why should I endanger my life and throw away the last six years of frustration? I thought it unwise to gamble away six years of a desperate fight for survival in the final hour. After much soul searching, I decided to follow my reasoning and intuition, and I did not go. I did, however, write a letter of explanation to the local command of the Committee of National Liberation, mentioning that, in accordance with my information, the war was just about over and there probably was not enough time left for me to attend the meeting and get back to my headquarters.

By military standards my response was certainly an act of insubordination. But we were partisans, and entirely different rules applied. Just in case, I took the necessary measures for my personal safety for the next few days. As it turned out, however, the precautions I took were not necessary.

The periodic visits from representatives of the Committee of National Liberation increased in frequency in direct proportion to the approaching end of the war. Their visits had a distinct political flavor, and some of the representatives, when alone with me, were quite candid about it. Their main concern was to prevent any one group from monopolizing the armed forces and so creating a nucleus for a potential future dictatorship. Most of these representative were people from the Liberal Party who did not want to fall into another trap such as took place there in the twenties. After these visits, the representatives left assured that my interest did not extend to either local or national Italian politics.

During the winter months preceding the end of the war, I had selected a group of two hundred young men and organized them into a temporary police force to prepare for the inevitable liberation of Savona. The existing police were compromised by their collaboration with the enemy. Although I had no experience in civil administration, I realized that a violent change-over would cause a breakdown of law and order, the consequences of which were dangerous for a community the size of Savona. I appointed my old friend Sergeant Noce, who had a military background, to head that group since he was the most likely to succeed in organizing them and giving them the proper training. Indeed, he had demonstrated his ability to maintain proper discipline as commander of the Third Brigade.

On April 25, 1945, the signal to liberate Savona came as scheduled. The day I had long wished for was finally at hand. The terrible nightmare was over.

The Nazis showed sense in surrendering immediately to the partisan security units, which had orders not to harm those who surrendered. But the diehards of the decomposing establishment—such as the Fascists and the Blackshirts—attempted to resist. They were too slow to realize that it was all over for them, and they barricaded themselves in the upper floors of downtown office buildings. Such obstacles were quickly overcome, however, and soon the Fascists inside the city were securely under lock and key.

After living with the Italians for several years and getting to know them closely, it was simply impossible for me to turn against any of them in hatred, irrespective of their recent activity. As a non-Italian by birth, I could not get completely involved in their personal problems but could act only as an impartial bystander. Nonetheless, while those Fascists were being brought to justice for committing crimes against humanity, I could not help but draw a comparison between their now miserable condition and my own situation of a not-too-distant past when I was hunted, not unlike a wild animal, only because I did not belong to the *Herrenvolk*.

As a rule people will do almost anything to save their lives. When the Fascists were brought in for questioning, I had to laugh at some of their attempts at disguise. The most comical was a man whose haste in peroxiding his dark hair left him with a head of blond hair with one of his eyebrows red and the other one black. Of course, even proper disguises were of no help to them, since most were local people and therefore well known to my men.

When they were later brought before a judge to answer for their misdeeds committed under the Nazi and Fascist regimes, almost no one was willing to help them. However, there was one lawyer who, using his superior courtroom skill and classical oratory, managed to save most of them from the firing squad. The irony was that he himself had been a victim of those imbeciles. One of the best attorneys in Savona, he had been brought down by the Fascist regime into an abyss of almost no return, yet now he managed to bring Ciceronian brilliance into full play in defense of his tormentors. I had first met him high up in the mountains just over two years before. It was the day I had returned from Mondovi after my unsuccessful attempt at contacting the partisans by way of my former boss Vigano. As we passed each other on a mountain path while coming from opposite directions, we looked at each other without expression. He said "Ciao," and I continued on my way after answering in kind. But I had a feeling that he had stopped. I turned my head to see him standing there, motioning for me to wait for him. Since I had no reason to fear only one man, I waited, but I kept my finger on the trigger as he approached. Noticing this, he assured me that he had only the best intentions. Still, I could not bring myself to trust him, and we parted company after that short encounter. Later on I met him again, but this time I was in a group with other partisans. He turned out to be a typical individualist and a liberal. In retrospect, I was glad that he never had been an official member of the partisan movement. Had this been the case, the discipline of a partisan would not have allowed him to defend his former enemies, and I would have been deprived of the privilege of being a witness to such a display of humanity. That memorable day proved a significant experience for me as a layman. Until I witnessed that attorney's performance in court, I would not have believed that a man could be capable of such selfless devotion to a profession.

The so-called interregnum lasted five days before the first Allied forces came into the city, and we were happy to see them, since their coming brought stability. I was then a police inspector of the city of Savona, with my office located at the Questura (police station). None of us in charge of the administration of the city and province had any prior experience in government as such, but we nevertheless managed to preserve peace and order. The boys demonstrated that they understood the responsibility we had placed on them, and I was convinced that their prior training and indoctrination for the job of public safety had clearly succeeded. For that, the greatest measure of credit goes to Sergeant Noce.

Several days after the Allies arrived, officials came from Rome and Genoa to take over some of the administrative jobs that required professional expertise. Since things had already settled down to a large extent, I felt strongly that from then on it was a matter for the local people to tend to their own store. However, at the insistence of my friends as well as the Allied command, I remained for a while longer.

Some of the minor Fascist cogs began to come out of hiding—in my opinion a bit too soon. Their appearance raised the blood pressure of the weather-beaten partisans, who, disturbed with such a turn of events, began to mistrust the Allied authorities. Despite this situation, a great majority of the partisans turned in their arms as requested. I personally supervised that operation, and we accomplished the job without delay or significant incident.

May 1 is a major holiday in many European countries. Even Adolph Hitler, in an effort to get the German working masses to swell his ranks, adopted May 1 as a national holiday in the Third Reich. For the partisans and the people of Savona, it was the first time they could celebrate real freedom since Mussolini's grab for power in 1922. From the early morning hours people began filling the city, which took on a festive air. All existing city organizations participated, as did all the partisans from the area around Savona. After the parades, the celebration climaxed at the main piazza in front of the monument to the fallen heroes of World War I.

I tried to stay away from what I thought to be an exclusively Italian affair, but I did not succeed. From two blocks away, I heard my name yelled in unison by the mass of men and women assembled in the piazza. "Enrico," they chanted over and over again. Someone knew where to find me, and disregarding my protest, they literally carried me through the streets, into a building, and out onto the second floor balcony where Colonel Zinnari was waiting for me. He promptly introduced me, but the roar of the crowd did not cease until they could see me. Then they applauded, and the whole mass of people began singing our song from the mountains. Almost all the boys were there. I could recognize their individual voices. I was by no means an orator, especially in a recently acquired language, but somehow I did manage to say a few words before leaving the balcony, genuinely moved by such an expression of respect and friendship. For several minutes afterward, the name "Enrico" still rang in my ears.

About two weeks after the final elimination of hostilities, a battalion of Italian regular armed forces from the Seventy-sixth Infantry Regiment of the Mantua Division came to Savona. Soon thereafter its commander, Colonel Giorgio Salvi, paid me a visit at my office in the Questura. With full cooperation from him, we arranged for a formal takeover of jurisdiction with all the fanfare usual on such occasions. On May 8, 1945, the two forces met at a large assembly, followed by a mass. After the open-air mass on the main piazza in Savona, right across from the World War I monument, Colonel Salvi and I together placed a wreath of flowers inside the wrought-iron enclosure surrounding the monument. Then, along with the city and province officials, the colonel and I reviewed a parade of our combined forces, and I gave a speech to the assembled crowd of some 35,000 people. I spoke from a second-floor balcony, as I had on May Day, but this time I had prepared my speech in advance. That was the last official military act of my partisan career.

Later, on May 19, I received a personal invitation from the commander of the Savona garrison, the same Colonel Salvi, to be his guest at a communion administered to his troops by the bishop of Savona, His Eminence Monsignor Pasquale Righetti.

As the situation slowly turned toward normal, things calmed down and people began to forget the troubles of the past. But instead of being absorbed in the general stream of daily life in such a serene place as Savona, with all the friends a man could desire, I felt in a kind of vacuum. I was overcome by restlessness; nothing mattered to me. In deference to my friends, I was compelled to keep my feelings from them. I did, however, share my thoughts with one man, a U.S. captain named Bernard Cahn, an attorney in civilian life who at the time was attached to the Allied Military Command in Savona. He had frequent contact with me in his official capacity as legal officer.

Captain Cahn invited me to attend a religious service with him in Genoa. A religious service is supposed to have a calming effect on the soul, and I am inclined to believe that this might be possible, depending on the nature and magnitude of one's problems and the particular atmosphere in which the service takes place. Also of prime importance is the subject matter and the individual who is responsible for creating the spiritual hegemony over such a varied gathering. My frame of mind was such that I perhaps expected, and maybe needed, something more than a simple religious ceremony to soothe my wounded soul. It has been said that people usually get out of something as much as they are willing to put into it. On the evening the service was to take place, I was prepared to invest everything of which I was capable, to offer my whole self in exchange for spiritual satisfaction. My effort, unfortunately, was of no avail.

After the minister completed the service, which he conducted in a dull, cut-and-dried manner, but seemingly to his own satisfaction, he turned to the small group and wished us well. He then led the group to the next room where refreshments and music were provided, and after everyone had eaten, he invited them to dance and be merry.

That was too much for me to swallow. I could have forgiven him for boring the congregation, and I saw nothing wrong with an honest attempt at entertainment of some kind, but the culmination of a religious service with a dance was an entirely different matter with me. I left in utter disgust, and my friend Captain Cahn, experiencing the same reaction, followed. Apparently those people didn't have a worry in the world. It was as if only the present counted; the horror of the past six years was of no importance to them anymore.

Under the influence of that evening, the experience of the last six years unfolded before me in its naked realism. On the way home, and for the next few days, I could concentrate on nothing else. I kept seeing the swollen faces of dying humans and the dried-out, quasi skeletons of the little boys and girls, whose eyes alone remained alive while they sat or lay half-naked in the snow, apparently numb beyond pain, in the filthy streets of the Warsaw ghetto. I remembered the young heroes who, at the risk of their own miserable lives, had crossed the ghetto wall into the forbidden sector of town to secure from some charitable Gentile a few frozen potatoes that they then tried to carry back into that hell on earth to feed their dear ones, thinking that if they could be sustained a few days more, they might survive that holocaust and see the hated tormentor destroyed.

Yes, that had been their hope. Whenever news from the front was good, it seemed too good to be true. Once in a while they would hear that the Nazis were in almost full retreat. But were they? If it seemed true, the ghetto residents would try again to survive with another few rotten potatoes, a piece of stale bread, or anything halfway digestible. But the young heroes, barely children yet with a stamina born of desperation, seldom succeeded in accomplishing their mission. Sometimes they were stopped, deprived of their hard-won victuals, severely beaten, and thrown back into the ghetto. Once I watched a boy manage to move a Nazi's heart enough to let him into the ghetto with his prized possessions, a few rotten potatoes, only to be stopped inside by a Jewish policeman who attempted to confiscate them. Fortunately the policeman was stopped by his Nazi counterpart when the boy's loud cries brought the confrontation to the Nazi's attention.

The sharp, penetrating smell of death had been everywhere. You could not escape it in the street. In the public parks, the bushes and trees seemed to exhale death fumes; they filled the air. Even the highways were full of the smell. If you happened to be in the vicinity of that slaughterhouse named Treblinka, you were subjected to the unusual smell of roasting humans. Dante's inferno would have been a rather poor substitute. Yes, a poor substitute indeed.

Yet I had no reason to be unhappy in Savona. I was on the city payroll as a police inspector, certainly a respectable position. For all practical purposes, my new life was equal to a vacation. But the old feeling of loneliness came back to me with ever-increasing pressure. Throughout the war I had never hesitated in making a decision, regardless of its importance, even when the safety of hundreds of men was at stake. Strange as it may sound, some of us evidently find it simpler to make decisions affecting other people's lives than to make those affecting our own. Nevertheless, a decision had to be made. Still, once a man decides to take to the road and move on, he has solved only half the problem. If moving was the proper thing to do, then to where?

Poland was a beautiful country, but the happy memories from the past were not sufficient to overcome the horrible experiences of recent times in which I had lost everything I cherished. Perhaps Germany, the land of my youth? The changes there had been far too drastic to let me feel comfortable in Germany again. Emotionally I was not prepared to live in either of those countries. I knew that I would have to get away from this part of the globe, as far away as possible and, more important, as quickly as I could.

Certificate of appreciation issued to the author by the British and Italian governments. The certificate reads, "Certificate to the Patriot. On behalf of the governments and the people of the United Nations we thank Hermann Vygoda for fighting the enemy on the battlefields, for joining the patriotic groups, for being among those men who carried arms for the triumph of freedom, for carrying out offensive operations, and for sabotaging and furnishing military information. With their bravery and faithfulness the Italian Patriots have contributed to the liberation of Italy and to the great cause of every free man. In the reborn Italy, the bearers of this certificate will be acclaimed as patriots who have fought for honor and freedom."

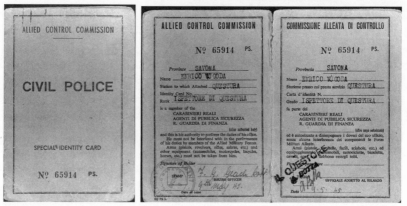

Identity cards issued to the author after the war. *Top:* Veteran's card. *Bottom:* Civil police card.

*Left:* Author's invitation to receive the Bronze Star Medal. *Below:* Author (third from right) moments after receiving the Bronze Star from U.S. General Mark Clark.

Hermann and Rae Wygoda in Chattanooga, Tennessee. *Right:* On their wedding day in 1947. *Below:* With their children on Hermann's fiftieth birthday in 1956; (L to R): Lois, Sylvia, Rae, Hermann, Mark.

Leon Peregal after the war. *Left:* In Davos, Switzerland, recuperating from injuries sustained during his escape from Italy in 1944. Photo courtesy of Paul Peregal. *Below:* With his wife Genissa and Hermann and Rae Wygoda at the 1967 World's Fair in Montreal, Canada.

Sylvia Wygoda representing her father in Savona in April 1995 at the celebration of the fiftieth anniversary of the liberation of the city by partisan forces (seated, right of center, with dignitaries from Savona and Rome). Photo by Pino Piccardo.

# 17    Finding a New Home

Throughout the war years, and particularly during the last two years of that struggle for survival, it did not dawn on me that there could be anything more to life than fighting the hated enemy, destroying as many of him as possible. Although the fighting was intense, and the unpleasant job of killing was frequent, the killing was by no means indiscriminate. We never lost sight of the fact that we were struggling for our own freedom, in concert with all those who fell victim to the savage, barbaric aggression of the abominable Nazi exterminating machine. We also kept in mind that not every German was a Nazi.

Neither I nor any of the men under my command ever suggested, thought of, or expected any compensation for the time spent in the mountains fighting the enemy. The conviction that our activities were contributing to the speedy demise of the Nazi war machine was sufficient incentive to fire our enthusiasm and increase our effort toward a final and decisive victory. Hence, it was completely unexpected news that we were to receive some recognition from the Allies as well as from the current Italian government.

I was notified to prepare the partisans of the Gin Bevilacqua Division and present them on a certain date at the Savona Opera House for a ceremony during which we were to receive a certificate of commendation from the Allied governments in recognition of our contribution to the war effort. In addition to getting the certificate, all the men were to receive monetary gifts as well. The last was the least expected.

Then, on June 25, 1946, I received a telegram from the Regional Military Command in Genoa ordering me to report to the Commando Generale del Corpo Volontari della Libertà, which was the supreme command of the entire partisan movement, located in Milan. There I was to obtain instructions concerning the receipt of an American decoration for valor. I was further advised to wear my official uniform at the ceremony, which was to take place the following day.

This new development caught me by surprise. Frankly, I could not comprehend why I had been selected for a decoration, since I was not aware of anything that I had done that would set me apart from any other commander in the Liguria military region. Despite my ignorance of the reason for the unexpected distinction, however, I was quite pleased. It was not until the following morning that I found out what type of decoration I was to be presented.

Later that day, in the beautiful courtyard of an ancient castle, with a military band providing appropriate music, General Mark Clark presented the American Bronze Star to ten partisans selected from the entire partisan movement of Italy, and I was one of those lucky few.

General Clark, then stationed in Vienna, had come down to Milan expressly for the presentation. The event had a special meaning for me. As English was one of the many languages with which I was unfamiliar, I did not understand what the general was saying, nor could I express my thanks to him for pinning that medal on my chest. But the thought that General Mark Clark could do this for me, could give me an American decoration when I had never seen his country, prompted me to select the United States of America as my new home. My thoughts were of an ancient Polish slogan, "Za wolnose nasza i wasza": for our freedom and yours as well.

# AFTERWORD

Frequently I have been asked my opinion of Germany, and particularly of the German people, regarding the tragic events of the last war in Europe. Although it would be rather presumptuous of me to think of myself as an expert in such a sensitive matter, the unusual nature of those events does call to question the validity of any so-called expert opinion if not based on personal experience.

The writers, directors, and actors who took part in that horrible drama were the Nazi hordes of Adolf Hitler and their victims, most of whom were Europeans, the majority of whom were Jews who either never came out of it alive or ended up physical and mental wrecks. Even those fortunate enough to live through that holocaust without being the inmates of a Nazi camp came close to suffering mental breakdowns.

The brutal excesses committed by the Nazis against innocent human beings during the war is by now common knowledge, despite the Nazis' desperate attempt to cover up their bloody work. Because the Nazis did not succeed in wiping out the traces of their crime, everyone was to see what some people were capable of doing to others.

Many books have already been written about this epochal event in our lifetime, and much more literature will be written on the subject for many years to come. All of it will finally be lost in the labyrinth of legends, and then fable, in not too many generations hence. I have found that some writers are quick to assume a rigid two-color attitude, a black-and-white approach. I do not believe, however, that those events were so simple as to disallow a variation in shades. If the matter were studied with an eye of objectivity, I venture that the color gray would be the broadest in the spectrum.

One group of writers is quick to assume an air of utter contempt for everything associated with the name of Germany, while the other surrounds everything German with nothing short of edelweiss flowers. The position taken by the first group is dangerous in many respects, because it allows the concept of collective guilt to be perpetuated.

Many times I wonder about my own attitude after living through so many ordeals, facing so many dangers, and seeing so many terrible things. But I have not brought myself to the point of hating the entire German people, because I have never believed in wholesale responsibility. Since my childhood I have been confronted with the accusation that the Jews, all Jews, were responsible for the crucifixion of Christ. The amazing thing is that at least some educated Christians believed this allegation. The clerics should have known better, and I am sure that some of them did; apparently, though, it was convenient for them to perpetuate such nonsense for reasons known only to themselves. It would be just as absurd to hold the entire German people responsible for crimes committed by a group of cutthroats and assassins.

Finally, it is my personal experience during that terrible war that prevents me from subscribing to the concept of collective guilt. I had the opportunity to hear staunch supporters of Hitler, as well as his enemies, express their criticism of the Nazis openly, loudly, and with strong words of discontent in Berlin's subways, streetcars, and public eating places. Whereas I could detect fear for the safety of the speaker in the faces of listeners, I saw no displeasure over the criticism of the regime. I experienced these events in Germany in 1943, a time when it took a great deal of courage for those people to speak out as they did. One need only recall Hitler's purge of his own friends in 1934 to understand the danger that such dissenters faced in Germany. Of course, these outspoken individuals were not necessarily in a majority, but they were indicative of opposition nonetheless. It is not hard to understand why heroes were not in the majority in Germany. No nation has ever had, or will ever have, many heroes.

Anyone who has lived with the Germans, shared their daily dreams and aspirations, and known the system under which the German people were raised and educated would not believe that they would revolt against established authority. The system under which the Germans had been trained was reminiscent of feudal times, during which the classical slave-and-master attitude prevailed. The accepted rule "Glaube und Gehorche" (Believe and Obey) was and still is the motto of the day. Such a motto is naturally conducive to letting someone else do the thinking. It would be meaningless to blame a people raised in such a fashion for not having revolted against the Nazi assassins before they gained too much power.

By and large, so little has changed in Germany since the unification of the different states into one entity that the pattern established then (1879) is basically the same today. The Weimar Republic (1919–33), which intervened for a few years, had been, I believe, no more than a nuisance to the ruling circles of Germany, who quickly overcame it. Only a short time passed before General von Hindenburg was elected president of the Republic, and once again the old ruling clique was in full control of the destiny of the Reich. This was a parody of democracy, since von Hindenburg was the embodiment of the oldest and most reactionary elements in Germany.

In the days after World War I, the reactionary forces of Germany proclaimed themselves to be the only bulwark against the spreading tide of communism; after World War II, they managed to convince the Western powers, particularly the United States, that they alone were the most reliable partners in the fight to save Western civilization from communism. By doing this, they not only retained their stranglehold on the German people, but they also avoided paying their debt to the people of the world for the hideous crimes they had committed. Some of those postwar rulers carried the horrible Nazi odor of the past: as early as the midsixties SS assassins were permitted to freely assemble in German cities under government protection. Unfortunately that odor spread over the entire body of the gullible and innocent German people.

Germany's rulers have often cited fictitious threats of invasion by Germany's neighbors as excuses both to launch invasions and to keep the German people in complete darkness about real issues. Equally so, the Nazis, with perfidy and fiction, conditioned the German people with regard to Jews and other Europeans. Their lurid propaganda of lies and slander against the Jewish population in Germany enabled the ruling circles to befuddle the mind of the average German, for whom they had nothing but contempt. Only when the Nazis decided to embark on international robbing expeditions did they suddenly discover brotherly love for the common man in Germany who, with his trusting outlook on life, was incapable of discerning the treachery. Although the German public was coerced into becoming partners in crime with the Nazis, they were not allowed to share in its fruits. In spite of all the wealth that the Nazis robbed from their millions of victims and shipped into the Reich, the German people remained poor as ever.

Those who promote the idea of collective guilt play into the hands of the Nazis by forcing the German people to take on a position of self-defense against being identified with Nazi crimes. Germans who promote this idea either miss the point altogether, since anyone who is constrained to apologize must by definition admit guilt, whether deserved or not, or they think they can mitigate their own share of responsibility by compromising the innocent. At the same time, those who postulate theories of collective guilt imply that even the victims are not entirely without blame. Such reasoning is, of course, preposterous.

# MEMORIAL FOR LEON PEREGAL
## Paul Peregal

After Hermann's arrest, Leon spent an uncomfortable morning, anxious about what had transpired. Nevertheless, he decided to turn up at work, hoping for the best. Any smattering of optimism was short-lived, however, for he was arrested while working at his desk.

Leon was held in detention and eventually jailed in the same building where Hermann was planning his escape. He managed to smuggle a metal file into his cell and took note of the crude bars covering the windows. He had no idea how long he would be locked up or what fate was in store for him. He could only assume the worst—that he would be taken away and shot. There was no time to lose. He proceeded to spend as much time as possible filing away at the fastenings, and over a few days had all but secured his port of departure. All that remained was an opportune moment.

During the day the Americans flew bombing sorties over Savona, and Leon observed that with each bombing run, the jail guards would flee for the security of some nearby bunkers. One day a group of laborers left the compound leaving a ladder conveniently leaning against the outside wall that surrounded the building. Leon decided that this was an auspicious time to make a break for it. It wasn't long before the drone of the bombers scattered the guards, allowing him to remove the disconnected bars and slip through the window. Between the building and the wall he scampered up the ladder, pulled it up and over the top of the wall, and used it to go down the other side. He headed out into the hills, walking and running as far as he could, until he came to a peasant farmhouse where he sought refuge with the family that lived there.

Leon spoke some Italian and, suffering from exhaustion and hunger, decided to reveal his story to these mountain folk. To his great relief, they fervently sympathized with his plight and hid him from the Germans for some time, until he had regained his strength and orientation. Eventually he realized that the only final escape route lay through the Alps and into Switzerland. He could count on the help of the Italian peasants, some of whom had partisan affiliations, but it would be a dangerous and grueling undertaking, pitting himself against the elements of nature.

The trek took its toll, and Leon suffered serious frostbite and contracted tuberculosis. But freedom was finally attained when he set foot on Swiss soil on June 4, 1944.

Leon spent over two years recuperating in a sanatorium in Davos, Switzerland. During this period he wrote an account of some of his wartime experiences, which included the years he was incarcerated in a German prisoner-of-war camp and his release into the Nazi maelstrom of Jewish persecution. In 1946 he received word from his only surviving sister (Dora) in Degendorf, a displaced person's camp, that their father and mother, Alexander and Ita, and younger sister and brother, Channa and Abrasha, all from Vilna, Poland, had been murdered by the Nazis.

It was some time before Leon was back on his feet and able to work. Listed with the International Refugee Organization, he was also granted a work permit and found employment in Bern for three years with Hasler A.G. Bern as a sign painter. Bern was an attractive and appealing city that offered a spirited social life to Leon, whose charming personality drew many friends. In 1951 he left Hasler for a position as a photographic laboratory technician with the Bern firm Foto-Zumstein. The Zumsteins were to become good friends of Leon's and faithfully corresponded with him long after he had moved to Canada.

While in Switzerland, Leon applied for visas to immigrate to the United States and Canada. But the vicissitudes of the war and the geopolitical realities of postwar Europe presented certain obstacles. Leon's health had stabilized, but his bout with tuberculosis greatly diminished his chances of becoming a candidate for immigration. The American consulate also requested an official birth certificate, which was unavailable since Vilna (Leon's birthplace) was in the hands of the recalcitrant Soviets. Nevertheless, glowing reports from affluent America and Canada—where careless individuals could develop serious back trouble from picking up all that money lying on the streets—inundated Leon from aunts, uncles, and cousins encouraging him not to relent. The day did indeed arrive when he received word from the Canadian Immigration Service in Bern that he had been granted an immigrant visa.

On August 4, 1952, Leon embarked on the SS *Argentina* from Genoa, and he arrived in Halifax, Nova Scotia, twelve days later. From there he went to stay with his cousins in Montreal and began the arduous process of cultural acclimatization and assimilation. English dominated the business community of Montreal in the fifties, and Leon was determined to add this language to his linguistic repertoire of Polish, German, Russian, Italian, and Yiddish. The time to do this became all too available when a serious recurrence of pulmonary tuberculosis landed him in a sanatorium in the Laurentian mountains north of Montreal for sixteen months. With his health restored, he was released in 1954 and returned to Montreal, where he devoted his energies to finding work. This was a demoralizing period for Leon. He found the winters unbearably cold and attributed his illness to the extremes of climate. Loneliness and unemployment weighed heavily on his spirits, and an unaccustomed pessimism set in. He was turned away time and again for lack of "Canadian work experience." No employer was prepared to endorse his European credentials. Living on a shoestring, he barely had carfare to make it to the interviews. In desperation he wrote to the Zumsteins, telling them of his plight, and contacted the Swiss authorities with the intention of returning to Switzerland. But fate intervened, and he finally secured a position as a draftsman rendering architectural concepts.

Before long Leon met my mother, Genissa Shainblum née Friedlander, a notarial stenographer who was born in Quebec City and who had an eight-year-old son—myself—from her previous marriage. In 1956 they were married, and eventually my adoption was legalized.

Leon was intent on pursuing his vocation as a photographic laboratory technician specializing in color processing and printing. After applying to several firms, he was hired and spent several years acquiring and improving his skills. For some time he operated his own commercial lab and studio with an emphasis on product photography. Later he joined the Photographic Services Department of the Canadian National Railways, where he helped pioneer the production of the first mural-sized color prints in Canada (these massive photographs, some of them more than twelve feet high and several yards long, were placed on revolving panels in Montreal's Canadian National Railways train station and advertised the scenic wonders of Canada). Leon also had a genius for invention and built various electronic devices to facilitate and enhance his photographic work.

A fine and dedicated father, he encouraged and fostered my artistic sensibilities, allowing me the freedom to evolve both as a person and as a painter. Leon's indomitable will to survive gave sustenance and inspiration to all those who knew him and took the time to listen to his story. Leon Peregal passed away on April 6, 1995.

# ENRICO REMEMBERED
## Sylvia Wygoda

Fifty years after Hermann "Enrico" Wygoda, commander of the Gin Bevilacqua Division of Italian partisans, brought freedom to the city of Savona, he was honored posthumously during the city's official celebration commemorating the fiftieth anniversary of liberation.

In a ceremony at the Teatro Comunale Chiabrera, a beautiful opera house in the center of Savona, my father's partisan name drew loud cheers and applause as the capacity audience heard the life story of the man who had become a hero to so many of them. Several generations of Italians learned from his daughter what most had never known before about the true identity of their respected and beloved *comandante*—that he was a Polish Jew whose family had perished under the same Nazi regime that had occupied their own city and killed and terrorized their families.

"Enrico," the humble hero, would have been amazed yet proud at the outpouring of genuine respect, admiration, and affection shown to his memory by partisans and citizens alike in April 1995.

In 1996 earth from Hermann Wygoda's grave was presented by partisan veterans during a mass to officials of Savona for burial in Savona's cemetery close to graves of the other brave partisans.

# INDEX

HERMANN WYGODA was a Polish Jew who survived the Holocaust. After living a covert life in Poland and Germany, he escaped to Italy, where he became a division commander in the Italian partisan army. Following the war, he was awarded the American Bronze Star for valor by Gen. Mark Clark of the U.S. Army. He wrote *In the Shadow of the Swastika* in Polish before emigrating to the United States in 1946; twenty years later, while self-employed as a building contractor in Tennessee, he translated this work into English. He died in Florida in 1982 at the age of seventy-five.

MARK WYGODA is the author's son. He has traveled widely giving illustrated presentations of his father's wartime experiences to educational, civic, and religious groups. He is a professor and head of the biology and environmental science department at McNeese State University and the author of several articles that have appeared in scientific journals. He lives in Lake Charles, Louisiana.

MICHAEL BERENBAUM, a prolific writer, lecturer, and teacher on the Holocaust, is an adjunct professor of theology at the University of Judaism in Los Angeles and formerly served as president and CEO of the Survivors of the Shoah Visual History Foundation. He is the author of many books, including *The World Must Know* and *After Tragedy and Triumph*.

DEBORAH KLEZMER is the author's granddaughter. A freelance writer and an editor of historical biographies, she currently serves as associate editor of the Women in World History series for Yorkin Publications and resides in Boston, Massachusetts.

SYLVIA WYGODA is the author's daughter. She is director of Holocaust Education for the State of Georgia and chairperson emeritus and executive director of the Georgia Commission on the Holocaust; she also is the producer and director of the award-winning video *Prejudice and Hate: Georgians and the Holocaust* and speaks on Holocaust issues. She resides in Atlanta, Georgia.

PAUL PEREGAL is an artist who lives and paints in Toronto, Canada. He is the son of Leon Peregal, who was the author's wartime companion.

The University of Illinois Press
is a founding member of the
Association of American University Presses.

University of Illinois Press
1325 South Oak Street
Champaign, IL 61820-6903
www.press.uillinois.edu